THE CRUSADES

Motives and Achievements

PROBLEMS IN EUROPEAN CIVILIZATION

THE
CRUSADES

Motives and Achievements

EDITED WITH AN INTRODUCTION BY

James A. Brundage

UNIVERSITY OF WISCONSIN — MILWAUKEE

D. C. HEATH AND COMPANY · BOSTON

Library of Congress Catalog Card number 64-15925

COPYRIGHT © 1964 BY D. C. HEATH AND COMPANY

Printed November 1967

Table of Contents

ORIGIN AND PURPOSES OF THE CRUSADES

ACHIEVEMENTS OF THE CRUSADES

Introduction

THE Crusades, as everyone agrees, were an important fact of medieval life. From 1095, when Pope Urban II (1088–99) proclaimed the first Crusade at the Council of Clermont, down to the sixteenth century, when Crusading, in a proper sense of the word, finally disappeared from European life, hundreds of thousands of people were involved in these expeditions. For fifteen generations of Europeans the Crusades were a living, vital part of their world. Thousands participated personally in one or more of these expeditions. Many thousands gave money to support one Crusade or another, while others prayed for them, fasted and did penance in the hope that they would be successful, and were indirectly affected by them in countless other ways.

Yet it has been difficult for historians to agree as to just what these expeditions were about, what they aimed to do, and how successful they were in accomplishing what they set out to do. In part, of course, this is a matter of emphasis. All historians who have dealt with the Crusades admit that, to some degree, there was in each of the Crusading expeditions an element of idealism — a belief that the conquest and protection of the Holy Places, particularly of the Holy Sepulchre at Jerusalem, was in itself a good and worthwhile task. There can have been very few Crusaders, if any, who rejected this view completely and who were wholly unaffected by it. Still, even in the period of the Crusades, there was widespread recognition of the equally evident fact that the protection of the Holy Places was not the sole aim of all who participated in the Crusades or even the main aim of many participants. One of the best-informed and most perceptive medieval historians of the Crusades, Archbishop William of Tyre (ca. 1130– ca. 1187), noted in his *History of Deeds Done Beyond the Sea* that "Not all of them, indeed, were there in behalf of the Lord. . . . Some were there so as not to desert their friends. Others were present lest they be thought idle, while others, still, were there out of frivolity or in order to escape their creditors, since they were loaded down with the obligations of many debts. All of them went for different reasons."

Still, recognizing the fact that not every Crusader was inspired by the same motives and that many individual Crusaders participated in the expeditions for a variety of reasons, there is a wide area of disagreement as to what the most important purposes of these expeditions were and what were the most significant reasons which led so many thousands of persons through so many hundreds of years to participate in them.

Thomas Fuller, a seventeenth-century English divine, was the first writer to deal with this problem at any length in English. In his *Historie of the Holy Warre,* Fuller re-stated the views of medieval and early modern writers on the origin and purposes of the Crusades in the form of a series of arguments for and against these expeditions, both as manifestations of political policy and as acts of religious zeal. Although Fuller was scrupulous to set forth both sides of the question, he was an argumentative Anglican clergyman writing in an age of violent religious polemic and he could not resist the temptation to use his discussion of the justification of the Crusades in order to voice some incidental denunciations of papal policy.

The historians of the Age of the Enlightenment in the eighteenth century generally emphasized in their accounts the crasser motives of the Crusaders and of those who planned and organized the expeditions. Voltaire summed up the driving motives of the Crusaders as "Religion, greed and restlessness." Gibbon emphasised in his account of the Crusades the opportunities which they furnished for spoils and for earthly, rather than supernatural, gains to the participants. It would be quite unrealistic to deny that there is some truth in these estimates. Yet the question remains, is this all there was to it? If so, one would think that there were sufficient opportunities to realize these objectives closer to home. Twelfth and thirteenth century Europe offered an abundance of outlets for greed and earthly gain on its eastern and southern frontiers. In central and eastern Europe and in Spain there was a wealth of opportunities for the ambitious, land-hungry warrior. Yet the Crusades in the Near East continued throughout this period to attract recruits by the thousands, despite the existence of easier opportunities for great gains with less trouble in Europe itself.

Twentieth century historians confronting the problem of explaining the Crusading phenomenon have been sharply divided in their views. American medievalists who have investigated the Crusades have tended to concern themselves very largely with the analysis of the interests and motives of the papacy in proclaiming the Crusades. Professor Dana Carleton Munro directed attention to the speech of Pope Urban II at Clermont in 1095, when he proclaimed the first Crusade. Munro's analysis of Urban's sermon at Clermont attempts to define the themes which the Pope dealt with and thus to discover the reasons which prompted Urban to initiate the first Crusade. Professor August C. Krey, a one-time student of Munro, focused his attention upon the ecclesiastical motives which underlay the Crusading movement. The paramount reason, in Krey's view, for the

decision to undertake the Crusade in the first place was the hope that these expeditions might be instrumental in securing a reunion of the Greek and Latin churches. Professor Frederic Duncalf who, like Krey, was also a pupil of Munro at Wisconsin, emphasised another facet of papal policy. In Duncalf's view, the major purpose underlying the proclamation of the Crusade was the hope of recapturing the Holy Land. As a secondary purpose of great importance he sees the aim of supporting and aiding the Byzantine Empire, which in 1095 had been hard hit by the Turkish conquest of Asia Minor in the previous two decades.

Other historians have taken the view that the aims and purposes of the Crusades cannot be adequately understood if they are viewed solely in the light of papal interests and designs. These historians have reasoned that a study of the popular response to papal appeals for the Crusading expeditions will furnish a deeper understanding of the Crusade phenomenon than will a study of papal policy alone. It was, after all, quite possible that Urban's call for the first Crusade at Clermont might not have produced any significant result at all. To understand how the Crusade came to fruition, we must understand what it was that attracted the masses who participated in these expeditions. So runs the argument. Louis Bréhier, in his influential book, *L'Église et l'orient au moyen âge*, emphasises in this connection the continuity of the Crusade with the pilgrimage tradition of the West. Bréhier views the Crusade as arising essentially out of the background of the pilgrimages to the Holy Land which Europeans had been making with some regularity for more than a thousand years prior to the beginning of the Crusades. During the latter part of the eleventh century, pilgrimage conditions had been rendered more hazardous as a result of the Turkish invasions of the Near East. At the same time, the influence of the Latins over the shrines of the Holy Land had diminished considerably. The response of Europeans to the call for a

Crusade is, in Bréhier's opinion, explicable largely in the light of this background.

Still other scholars have sought to explain the response which the Crusade attracted in terms of popular ideology. Paul Rousset's investigations have led him to the conclusion that the strong currents of anti-Muslim feeling which he finds in contemporary literature reflect the ideology of the masses who flocked to the Crusading banners. The response to the Crusade, in his estimation, may best be accounted for in the light of the hostility of Europeans toward Islam. It is only this which can satisfactorily explain the enthusiasm which greeted the call for Crusading warriors and the vigor with which the early Crusades were prosecuted. In a similar vein, Professor Norman Cohn also emphasizes the importance of the emotional impact of the call to the Crusade on the masses who heard and responded to it. He goes beyond Rousset in linking the response to the Crusading message with the eschatological currents of eleventh and twelfth century Christian religious thought.

Another approach to the problem of understanding the appeal of the Crusade to large numbers of medieval people is exemplified by Walter Porges' essay on "The Clergy, the Poor and the Non-Combatants on the First Crusade." Porges tries to analyse the composition of the Crusading army of 1096–99 and to deduce the objectives of the masses of the participants from the chroniclers' accounts of their actions on the expedition. Although he is concerned with accounts of actions primarily, rather than with expressions of attitudes and opinions (which are emphasized by Rousset and Cohn), Porges arrives at conclusions which are very similar to theirs in many respects.

This emphasis, in turn, has been questioned by historians who attribute greater significance to other factors in the genesis of the Crusades. Professor J. J. Saunders, for one, argues in his essay on "The Idea of a Holy War" that the Crusades may best be seen as one of the results of the papacy's efforts to harness the machinery of feudalism to the service of the Church.

Economic historians of the middle ages, such as Professor Hilmar Krueger, view the Crusades in another light altogether. To economic historians the Crusades are most intelligible if viewed as an episode in the expansion of Europe which began in the eleventh and twelfth centuries. The Crusading expeditions represent only one front in a much larger expansionist movement which led Western Europeans in this period to seek to establish control over many different regions. Likewise, the economic historians of the middle ages have been much impressed with the opportunities which Crusading offered for material gain. Here the Italian merchant cities, such as Genoa, Pisa, and Venice, played an especially significant role. On the one hand, they assisted the Crusading armies in their conquests in the Near East, while on the other hand the success of the early Crusading expeditions in establishing Western control over several of the important seaport towns of the eastern Mediterranean contributed heavily to the prosperity of the Italian cities and merchants.

Other historians, represented in these selections by Professor A. S. Atiya, have chosen to view the Crusades in terms of the long-range political antagonisms of East and West in the Mediterranean basin. For Professor Atiya the Crusades are essentially the "Frankish Solution of the Eastern Question in mediaeval times." It was a solution which failed of success. The West was unable to secure more than a short-lived control of a few portions of the eastern Mediterranean coast and was unable to impose its control on this area permanently. As Professor Atiya sees it, the unsuccessful "Frankish Solution" was answered by the "Islamic Solution" — a Muslim counter-Crusade, which resulted in the imposition of a long-standing Muslim hegemony upon the Holy Land and much of the rest of the eastern Mediterranean as well.

Estimates of the "success" or "failure" of

the Crusades have naturally varied with historians' conclusions about the aims and objectives which motivated these expeditions. Writers of an older generation, such as Archer and Kingsford, were generally much more generous in their estimation of the importance of the Crusades and of their contributions to Western European life than more recent writers have been. Professor Arnold Toynbee, who measures the achievement of the Crusades in the light of his supposition that they were principally wars of expansion, finds them a military failure. His analysis of the Crusading movement concentrates on the reasons which underlay its military failures and, conversely, the reasons for the military successes of its opponents.

Sir Steven Runciman, summing up his three-volume *History of the Crusades*, also concludes that the Crusading movement was a failure, but he counts it primarily a moral failure. He contrasts the alleged objectives of the Crusading armies with the cruelty, intolerance, greed, and cynicism, of many of their actions. The whole enterprise, Runciman concludes, was a "vast fiasco," "a long act of intolerance in the name of God, which is the sin against the Holy Ghost."

To an earlier writer, Edward Gibbon, the Crusades were an ironic success — a triumph of superstition and barbarism, made possible by the savage fanaticism of the Crusaders themselves. Out of the enormous efforts which were made to conquer the East came only some small incidental gains for Western Europeans in their own homelands. Chief among these gains was the undermining of feudalism as a result of the Crusading enterprises which sapped the strength and the resources of the feudal nobility.

Professor Louis Bréhier, however, makes a more positive assessment of the achieve-

ments of the Crusades. Viewing the Crusades as wars of defence against Islam, Bréhier concludes that they succeeded in their objective. He points out that during the five centuries when Europeans were more or less continuously engaged in Crusading, the tide of Muslim advance toward the West was stopped, only to be resumed as the Crusades gradually lost their appeal to Western Europeans at the close of the middle ages. Furthermore, Bréhier points to another facet of the Crusading movement. The Crusades left behind, he believes, a heritage of idealism which has not yet ceased to influence Western man and which has had important influences reaching far beyond the actual Crusading expeditions themselves.

What can be gathered from these various and seemingly contradictory appraisals of the Crusading movement? Should we perhaps relapse into a kind of historical agnosticism and conclude that, where there is so much disagreement among scholars, no conclusion is possible? Or should we, instead, affect a syncretistic approach by concluding that there may be much in all of these varying attempts to explain the phenomenon and that we will accept each of them as a partial answer to the problem?

Either of these approaches is possible. Both of them appear to resolve the problem — one by avoiding a conclusion and the other by avoiding the difficulty of making a choice between differing conclusions. Both of them also avoid the necessity of exercising judgment.

A third and better alternative is at once more difficult and more instructive. It involves a careful analysis and evaluation of these varied estimates of the objectives and the achievements of the Crusades. It is only in this way that a responsible and mature judgment can be formed on this, or any other, historical problem.

CHRONOLOGY OF THE CRUSADES

638	Muslim conquest of Jerusalem
1054	Schism of the Greek and Latin Churches
1095	Council of Clermont: Pope Urban II proclaims the First Crusade
1099	Capture of Jerusalem by the First Crusade; Latin Kingdom of Jerusalem established
1144	Latin County of Edessa falls to the Muslims
1146–48	Second Crusade; attack on Damascus
1169–93	Saladin ruler of Egypt and Syria
1187–89	Saladin captures Jerusalem; Latin states wiped out
1189–92	Third Crusade; Latin states restored
1202–04	Fourth Crusade; Byzantine Empire attacked by Crusaders; Constantinople falls
1204–61	Latin Empire of Constantinople
1208–29	Albigensian Crusade
1212	Children's Crusade
1218–21	Fifth Crusade; attack on Egypt
1227–29	Crusade of Frederick II; Jerusalem regained
1239	Egyptians recapture Jerusalem
1243–60	Mongol attacks on Near Eastern Muslim powers
1248–54	Crusade of Saint Louis, King of France; attack on Egypt
1268–91	Egyptian attacks on Latin states
1270	Saint Louis' Crusade against Tunis
1270–72	Crusade of King Edward I of England
1276	King of Jerusalem retires to Cyprus
1291	Fall of Acre, last major Crusader stronghold in Palestine
1309	Knights Hospitallers occupy Rhodes
1365	Crusade of King Peter I of Cyprus
1365–66	Crusade of Amadeus VI, Count of Savoy
1390	Crusade of Louis II, Duke de Bourbon, against Tunis
1396	Crusade of Nicopolis against the Turks
1444	Crusade of Varna against the Turks
1523	Rhodes captured by the Turks
1570	Cyprus taken by the Turks

The Conflict of Opinion

MOTIVES OF THE CRUSADES

"[It appears] that, however much Urban [II] desired the other objectives of the Crusade, his chief aim was to bring about the union of the Greek and Latin Churches under the headship of the bishop of Rome."

— A. C. KREY

"The pope, then, gave the crusade two aims: the recovery of the Holy Land, and the deliverance of the eastern Christians."

— FREDERIC DUNCALF

"[The Crusade] is in reality a spontaneous expression of the enthusiasm for the Holy Land which two centuries of uninterrupted pilgrimages and memories of the greatness of Charlemagne had impressed on the hearts of Western Christendom."

— LOUIS BRÉHIER

"Although the possibility of recapturing [Jerusalem] seems to have played little part in Urban's original plan, it was this prospect that intoxicated the masses of the poor. In their eyes the Crusade was an armed and militant pilgrimage, the greatest and most sublime of pilgrimages."

— NORMAN COHN

"The Crusades were part of a pan-European expansionist movement that pushed into all directions, partially under the impetus or guise of Christianity."

— HILMAR C. KRUEGER

"Consequently, we may deduce in all simplicity that the Crusades in their technically limited sense were merely the Frankish solution of the Eastern Question in medieval times."

— A. S. ATIYA

"The Crusades were then primarily wars of an idea, and it is this that sets them apart from all other wars of religion; for into the Crusades proper the spirit of religious intolerance or sectarian jealousy hardly entered."

— T. A. ARCHER and C. L. KINGSFORD

ACHIEVEMENTS OF THE CRUSADES

"In the long sequence of interaction and fusion between Orient and Occident out of which our civilization has grown, the Crusades were a tragic and destructive episode."

— Sir Steven Runciman

"Our findings may be summed up in the verdict that the Medieval Western Christian competitors for dominion over the Mediterranean Basin were neither strong enough to subdue their neighbours nor cultivated enough to captivate them."

— Arnold J. Toynbee

"The Crusades were the strongest influence on the development of medieval trade and industry."

— Hilmar C. Krueger

"It would be unjust to condemn out of hand these five centuries of heroism which had such fertile results for the history of Europe and which left behind in the consciences of modern peoples a certain ideal of generosity and a taste for sacrifice in behalf of noble causes which the harshest lessons of reality will never erase completely."

— Louis Bréhier

ORIGIN AND PURPOSES OF THE CRUSADES

The Crusades: What Was Their Justification?

THOMAS FULLER

Thomas Fuller, D.D. (1608–1661), was a seventeenth-century English historian whose *Historie of the Holy Warre* was the first widely read English account of the Crusades. Educated at Queens' College, Cambridge, Fuller held various appointments in the Anglican Church during his career and, in addition, wrote both polemical and historical treatments of a variety of subjects. His treatment of the lawfulness of the Crusades recapitulates the classical arguments for and against these expeditions to the East.

ARGUMENTS FOR THE LAWFULNESSE OF THE HOLY WARRE

It is stiffely canvased betwixt learned men, whether this warre was lawfull or not. The reasons for the affirmative are fetcht either from piety or policie: And of the former sort are these:

1. All the earth is Gods land let out to tenants; but Judea was properly his demesnes, which he kept long in his own hands for himself and his children. Now though the infidels had since violently usurped it, yet no prescription of time could prejudice the title of the King of Heaven, but that now the Christians might be Gods champions to recover his interest.

2. Religion bindeth men to relieve their brethren in distresse, especially when they implore their help, as now the Christians in Syria did; whose intreaties in this case, sounded commands in the ears of such as were piously disposed.

3. The Turks by their blasphemies and reproaches against God and our Saviour, had disinherited and divested themselves of all their right to their lands; and the Christians, as the next undoubted heirs, might seize on the forfeiture.

4. This warre would advance and increase the patrimony of Religion, by propagating the Gospel, and converting of infidels. If any object that Religion is not to be beaten into men with the dint of the sword; yet it may be lawfull to open the way by force, for instruction, catechising, and such other gentle means to follow after.

5. The beholding of those sacred places in Palestine would much heighten the adventurers devotion, and make the most frozen heart to melt into pious meditations.

6. This enterprise was furthered by the perswasions of sundry godly men, S. Bernard, and others. Now though a lying spirit may delude the prophets of Achab, yet none will be so uncharitable as to think God would suffer his own Michaiah to be deceived.

7. God set his hand to this warre and approved it by many miracles which he wrought in this expedition, and which are so confidently and generally reported by credit-worthy writers that he himself is a miracle that will not believe them.

Neither want there arguments derived from policie.

From Thomas Fuller, *The Historie of the Holy Warre* (Cambridge: Thomas Buck, 1639), pp. 13–16.

1

1. Palestine was a parcell of the Romane Empire, though since won by the Saracens: and though the Emperour of Constantinople could not recover his right, yet did he always continue his claim, and now (as appeared by his letters read in the Placentine Councel) Alexius requested the Princes of the West to assist him in the recovery thereof.

2. A preventive warre grounded on a just fear of an invasion is lawfull: But such was this Holy Warre. And because most stresse is laid on this argument, as the main supporter of the cause, we will examine and prove the parts thereof.

Though umbrages and light jealousies created by cowardly fancies be too narrow to build a fair quarrel on; yet the lawfulnesse of a preventive warre founded on just fear, is warranted by reason and the practice of all wise nations. In such a case it is folly to do as country-fellows in a fense-school, never ward a blow till it be past: but it is best to be before-hand with the enemie, lest the medicine come too late for the maladie. In such dangers to play an after-game is rather a shift than a policie: especially seeing warre is a tragedy which alwayes destroyeth the stage whereon it is acted; it is the most advised way, not to wait for the enemie, but to seek him out in his own countrey.

Now that the Mahometans (under whom the Turks and Saracens are comprehended, differing in nation, agreeing in religion and spite against Christians) were now justly to be feared, cannot be denied. So vast was the appetite of their sword, that it had alreadie devoured Asia, and now reserved Grecia for the second course. The Bosporus was too narrow a ditch, and the Empire of Grecia too low an hedge to fense the Pagans out of West-Christendome: yea, the Saracens had lately wasted Italy, pillaged and burned many churches neare Rome itself, conquered Spain, inroded Aquitain, and possessed some islands in the mid-land-sea. The case therefore standing thus, this Holy Warre was both lawfull and necessarie: which like unto a sharp pike in the bosse of a buckler, though it had a mixture of offending, yet it was chiefly of a defensive nature, to which all preventive warres are justly reduced.

Lastly, this warre would be the sewer of Christendome, and drain all discords out of it. For active men like mill-stones in motion, if they have no other grist to grind, will set fire one on another. Europe at this time surfeited with people, and many of them were of stirring natures, who counted themselves undone when they were out of doing; and therefore they employed themselves in mutual warres and contentions: But now this Holy Warre would make up all breaches, and unite all their forces against the common foe of Christianitie.

REASONS AGAINST THE HOLY WARRE

Yet all these reasons prevail not so forcibly, but that many are of the contrary opinion, and count this warre both needlesse and unlawfull, induced thereunto with these or the like arguments.

1. When the Jews were no longer Gods people, Judea was no longer Gods land by any particular appropriation; but on the other side, God stamped on that country an indelible character of desolation, and so scorched it with his anger, that it will never change colour, though Christians should wash it with their bloud. It is labour in vain therefore for any to endeavour to re-establish a flourishing kingdome in a blasted countrey: and let none ever look to reap any harvest, who sow that land which God will have to lie fallow.

2. Grant that the Turks were no better than dogs, yet were they to be let alone in their own kennel. They and the Saracens their predecessors, had now enjoyed Palestine foure hundred and sixty yeares: Prescription long enough to sodder the most crackt title, and not onely to corroborate but to create a right. Yea, God himself may seem herein to allow their title, by suffering them so long peaceably to enjoy it.

3. To visit those places in Jerusalem (the theatre of so many mysteries and miracles) was as uselesse as difficult; and might be

superstitious if any went (as it is to be feared too many did) with placing transcendent holinesse in the place, and with a wooden devotion to the materiall Christ. The Angel sent the women away from looking into the sepulchre, with *He is risen, he is not here* (Matt. 28:6); and thereby did dehort them and us, from burying our affections in Christs grave, but rather to seek him where he was to be found. At this day a gracious heart maketh every place a Jerusalem where God may as well and as acceptably be worshipped. S. Hilarion though he lived in Palestine saw Jerusalem but once, and then onely because he might not seem to neglect the holy places for their nearnesse and vicinitie. And S. Hierome (though himself lived at Bethlehem) diswaded Paulinus from coming thither; for the pains would be above the profit.

4. Lastly, this warre was a quicksand to swallow treasure, and of a hot digestion to devoure valiant men: no good, much evil came thereby; and the Christians that went out to seek an enemie in Asia, brought one thence, to the danger of all Europe and the losse of a fair part thereof. For though, *Careat successibus opto* [May he never speed] *Quisquis ab eventu facta notanda putet* [Who from the issue censures of the deed], and though an argument fetcht from the successe is but a cyphre in itself, yet it increaseth a number when joyned with others.

These reasons have moved the most moderate and refined Papists and all Protestants generally in their judgments to fight against this Holy Warre. But as for the opinion of Bibliander (who therein stands without company) if Bellarmine hath truly reported it, it is as farre from reason as charity; namely, that these Christians that went to fight against the Saracens, were the very army of Gog and Magog spoken of by the prophet Ezeckiel. Yet must we not here forget that such as went at this time to Jerusalem (whether ridiculously or blasphemously, or both, let others judge) did carry a goose before them, pretending it to be the holy Ghost.

Motives of the Crusaders

EDWARD GIBBON

Edward Gibbon, born at Putney in 1737, was one of England's greatest historians. His *Decline and Fall of the Roman Empire*, first published between 1776 and 1788, remains a landmark in historical writing on the middle ages. Gibbon's viewpoint is that of an "enlightened" English rationalist. He died in 1794.

THE cold philosophy of modern times is incapable of feeling the impression that was made on a sinful and fanatic world [by the proclamation of the Crusades]. At the voice of their pastor, the robber, the incendiary, the homicide, arose by thousands to redeem their souls by repeating on the infidels the same deeds which they had exercised against their Christian brethren; and the terms of atonement were eagerly embraced by offenders of every rank and denomination. None were pure; none were exempt from the guilt and penalty of sin; and those who were the least amenable to the justice of God and the church were the best entitled to the temporal and eternal recompense of their pious courage. If they fell, the spirit of the Latin clergy did not hesitate to adorn their tomb with the crown of martyrdom; and should they survive, they could expect without impatience the delay and increase of their heavenly reward. They offered their blood to the Son of God, who had laid down his life for their salvation: they took up the cross, and entered with confidence into the way of the Lord. His providence would watch over their safety; perhaps his visible and miraculous power would smooth the difficulties of their holy enterprise. The cloud and pillar of Jehovah had marched before the Israelites into the promised land. Might not the Christians more reasonably hope that the rivers would open for their passage; that the walls of the strongest cities would fall at the sound of their trumpets; and that the sun would be arrested in his mid-career, to allow them time for the destruction of the infidels?

Of the chiefs and soldiers who marched to the holy sepulchre, I will not dare to affirm that *all* were prompted by the spirit of enthusiasm, the belief of merit, the hope of reward, and the assurance of divine aid. But I am equally persuaded that in *many* it was not the sole, that in *some* it was not the leading principle of action. The use and abuse of religion are feeble to stem, they are strong and irresistible to impel, the stream of national manners. Against the private wars of the barbarians, their bloody tournaments, licentious loves, and judicial duels, the popes and synods might ineffectually thunder. It is a more easy task to provoke the metaphysical disputes of the Greeks, to drive into the cloister the victims of anarchy or despotism, to sanctify the patience of slaves and cowards, or to assume the merit of the humanity and benevolence of modern Christians. War and exercise were the reigning passions of the Franks or Latins; they were enjoined, as a penance, to gratify those passions, to visit distant lands, and to draw their swords against the nations of the East. Their victory, or even their attempt, would immortalise the names of the intrepid heroes of the cross; and the purest piety could not be insensible to the

From Edward Gibbon, *The Decline and Fall of the Roman Empire*, VI, ed. J. B. Bury (London, 1898), pp. 270–275.

most splendid prospect of military glory. In the petty quarrels of Europe, they shed the blood of their friends and countrymen, for the acquisition perhaps of a castle or a village. They could march with alacrity against the distant and hostile nations who were devoted to their arms; their fancy already grasped the golden sceptres of Asia; and the conquest of Apulia and Sicily by the Normans might exalt to royalty the hopes of the most private adventurer. Christendom, in her rudest state, must have yielded to the climate and cultivation of the Mahometan countries; and their natural and artificial wealth had been magnified by the tales of pilgrims and the gifts of an imperfect commerce. The vulgar, both the great and small, were taught to believe every wonder, of lands flowing with milk and honey, of mines and treasures, of gold and diamonds, of palaces of marble and jasper, and of odiferous groves of cinnamon and frankincense. In this earthly paradise each warrior depended on his sword to carve a plenteous and honourable establishment, which he measured only by the extent of his wishes. Their vassals and soldiers trusted their fortunes to God and their master: the spoils of a Turkish emir might enrich the meanest follower of the camp; and the flavour of the wines, the beauty of the Grecian women, were temptations more adapted to the nature, than to the profession, of the champions of the cross. The love of freedom was a powerful incitement to the multitudes who were oppressed by feudal or ecclesiastical tyranny. Under this holy sign, the peasants and burghers, who were attached to the servitutde of the glebe, might escape from an haughty lord, and transplant themselves and their families to a land of liberty. The monk might release himself from the discipline of his convent; the debtor might suspend the accumulation of usury and the pursuit of his creditors; and outlaws and malefactors of every cast might continue to brave the laws and elude the punishment of their crimes.

These motives were potent and numer-

ous: when we have singly computed their weight on the mind of each individual, we must add the infinite series, the multiplying powers of example and fashion. The first proselytes became the warmest and most effectual missionaries of the cross: among their friends and countrymen they preached the duty, the merit, and the recompense of their holy vow; and the most reluctant hearers were insensibly drawn within the whirlpool of persuasion and authority. The martial youths were fired by the reproach or suspicion of cowardice; the opportunity of visiting with an army the sepulchre of Christ was embraced by the old and infirm, by women and children, who consulted rather their zeal than their strength; and those who in the evening had derided the folly of their companions were the most eager, the ensuing day, to tread in their footsteps. The ignorance, which magnified the hopes, diminished the perils, of the enterprise. Since the Turkish conquest, the paths of pilgrimage were obliterated; the chiefs themselves had an imperfect notion of the length of the way and the state of their enemies; and such was the stupidity of the people that, at the sight of the first city or castle beyond the limits of their knowledge, they were ready to ask, whether that was not the Jerusalem, the term and object of their labours. Yet the more prudent of the crusaders, who were not sure that they should be fed from heaven with a shower of quails or manna, provided themselves with those precious metals which, in every country, are the representatives of every commodity. To defray, according to their rank, the expenses of the road, princes alienated their provinces, nobles their lands and castles, peasants their cattle and the instruments of husbandry. The value of property was depreciated by the eager competition of multitudes; while the price of arms and horses was raised to an exorbitant height, by the wants and impatience of the buyers. Those who remained at home, with sense and money, were enriched by the epidemical disease: the sovereigns acquired at a cheap rate the domains of their vassals; and the ecclesiastical purchasers completed the payment by the assurance of their prayers. The cross, which was commonly sewed on the garment, in cloth or silk, was inscribed by some zealots on their skin; an hot iron, or indelible liquor, was applied to perpetuate the mark; and a crafty monk, who showed the miraculous impression on his breast, was repaid with the popular veneration and the richest benefices of Palestine.

Papal Proclamation of the Crusade

DANA CARLETON MUNRO

Dana Carleton Munro was born at Bristol, Rhode Island, in 1866. As Professor of History, first at the University of Wisconsin and later at the University of Pennsylvania and at Princeton, Munro became the founder of what has come to be known as the American school of historians of the Crusades. He planned for many years to write a comprehensive history of the Crusades, but his own high standards of historical scholarship and his many commitments to other projects prevented him from completing more than a few articles and some preliminary drafts for the great history which he planned. After Munro's death in 1933, Professor A. C. Krey, a former student of his, prepared the material which Munro had assembled for his projected history into a book which was published in 1935 as *The Kingdom of the Crusaders*. In addition to the material in that book, Munro published several shorter studies in the history of the Crusades, of which this article is one.

THE belief that Peter the Hermit was the instigator of the first crusade has long been abandoned. To Pope Urban II. belongs the credit, or the responsibility, for the movement. On November 27, 1095, at the Council of Clermont, he delivered the address which led so many thousands to take the cross. There are several versions of this speech, but it cannot be proved that any one of them was written until a number of years after the Council. As these differ decidedly in their expressions, it has been assumed that it is impossible to determine what the pope actually said. It is the purpose of this paper to show by an examination of the various versions that, in spite of the verbal differences, there is a remarkable agreement among the contemporary reporters, and consequently that it is possible to ascertain the subjects which the pope discussed.

The important versions are given by Fulcher of Chartres, Robert the Monk, Baldric of Dol, Guibert of Nogent, and William of Malmesbury. Those of William of Tyre, Ordericus Vitalis, Roger of Wendover, and others are . . . of little importance.

Fulcher of Chartres, in his *Historia Iherosolymitana*, gives a very brief account of Urban's exhortation. But he prefaces it by a summary of the pope's speech relative to the evil conditions in the West. This was an address to the clergy who were at the Council. At its close the Truce of God was proclaimed and all who were present promised to observe it. . . . Then Urban began his exhortation. This is the portion of Fulcher's account which must be compared with the versions given by the others. . . .

Robert the Monk, in his *Historia Iherosolymitana*, gives a somewhat longer account. He states in his preface that he was commissioned to write the history because he was at Clermont. It is not possible to determine the time when he wrote; certainly it was not before 1101–1102; probably it was a few years later. He does not have the first speech of Urban to the clergy, but he does give a summary of the pope's second speech to the clergy, after the completion

From Dana Carleton Munro, "The Speech of Pope Urban II at Clermont, 1095," in *The American Historical Review*, XI (January, 1906), pp. 231–242. Reprinted with permission of the American Historical Association.

of his exhortation. This portion of his account should be omitted in comparing it with the other versions. His version has frequently been preferred by later historians.

Baldric of Bourgueil, archbishop of Dol, probably wrote his *Historia Jerosolimitana* shortly after 1107. He states in two different passages that he was at the Council. He does not give the first speech of Urban to the clergy, but has a brief summary of the second. . . .

Guibert, abbot of Nogent, wrote the first portion of his *Gesta Dei per Francos* not later than 1108. . . . Guibert knew Fulcher's *Historia* and used it for the later portions of his work, but he did not copy Fulcher's version of the speech. His report differs decidedly from those given by the others. He makes no mention of either address to the clergy.

William of Malmesbury, although a contemporary, did not write his version until thirty or more years after the Council. It has been regarded as of little value. Hagenmeyer and Röhricht state that it is based upon Fulcher's account. This is true for portions but not for the whole of William's version. He has some points that he could not have drawn from Fulcher. He says that his informants were persons who had heard the speech. There seems to be no more reason for doubting this than any other uncorroborated statement, and his version ought certainly to be considered. The other reports of the speech are obviously copied or fictitious. To the latter class belongs the speech in William of Tyre, which has so often been regarded as the most correct version. It has no independent value.

The reconstruction of the exhortation must be based upon the versions of Robert and Baldric, who say that they were at Clermont; of Fulcher and Guibert, who may have been present; and of William of Malmesbury, who says that his information was derived from persons who were present. All, except Fulcher, state that they do not reproduce the exact words of the pope. All that can be attempted, therefore,

is a reconstruction of the outline of the exhortation.

This reconstruction is somewhat difficult inasmuch as the three separate speeches of the pope have been confused to some extent in the different versions. The task of reconstruction seems to be further complicated by the existence of points of resemblance between some versions of the speech and passages in the famous letter of the Emperor Alexius to Count Robert of Flanders. The genuineness and date of the letter have long been subjects of controversy. . . .

It is to be noted, however, that if the letter was a source, no one in his version used it for more than a few points, and in each case other accounts of the speech mention these same points in a manner that shows no influence of the letter. Consequently it seems almost certain that these subjects were mentioned by the pope, and hence the letter need not be considered in the analysis. It is not necessary, either, to discuss the question whether Urban was influenced by the letter or whether, on the other hand, the letter was based upon Urban's speech. It seems probable that the letter, whichever date is taken for its composition, was in existence before any of the versions which have parallel passages; and that the writers of these used it. Believing that Urban discussed a subject, it would be the most natural thing for Robert or Baldric or William to borrow from any source at hand either a pertinent account or a phrase which struck his fancy. This was such a common practice in the middle ages that it would have been remarkable if they had not done it. The letter, therefore, probably influenced the mode of expression in some versions, but not the general outline.

In order to ascertain what Pope Urban actually said it is now necessary to analyse each version of the speech, and to ascertain the separate facts given in each. It is to be expected *a priori* that the ideas will be expressed in different words and that each writer will dwell upon the portions of greatest interest to him, passing lightly over other portions. After such an analysis, it will be possible to select the facts which seem to be well vouched for and thus to determine the main outline of the pope's remarks. Accordingly the separate facts will now be taken up; those given in Fulcher's version will be used first; and in each case it will be noted when the same fact is cited by any of the others. Then the other speeches will be analysed in the same manner, and in the following order: Robert, Baldric, Guibert, William of Malmesbury.

Necessity of aiding the brethren in the East. Found in all.

Appeals for aid from the East. Found in Fulcher, Robert, and possibly in Baldric. Guibert does not mention these appeals in his account of the speech, but refers, in the preceding chapter, to the gifts and prayers of the emperor by which Urban was moved. This point is not referred to by William of Malmesbury.

Victorious advance of the Turks. Mentioned by Fulcher and Robert. Baldric and Guibert have no such explicit mention, but all the earlier portions in each of their speeches presupposes the knowledge of such a conquest. On the other hand, William of Malmesbury has a long list of the provinces which the Turks had conquered.

Sufferings of the Christians in the East. Mentioned very briefly by Fulcher, dwelt upon at great length by Robert, to a lesser degree by Baldric and William. Guibert does not mention this subject, but does dwell upon the sufferings of the pilgrims.

Desecration or destruction of the churches and holy places. Mentioned by Fulcher, by Robert, at great length by Baldric, and slightly by William. Guibert also mentions this, but treats it under the special sanctity of Jerusalem.

This is God's work. Mentioned explicitly by Fulcher; it is, in fact, the underlying thought in all the versions. . . .

Rich and poor alike ought to go. Mentioned by Fulcher, but not explicitly by the others. It seems probable that Urban aroused even greater enthusiasm than he desired. In his second address to the clergy he stated that he did not desire old men, or those unfitted for war, or women without guardians. Clerks were not to go without the permission of their bishop, nor laymen without the blessing of their priest. These same limitations are brought out later in the letter of Urban to the inhabitants of Bologna. But the pope's eloquence had been too persuasive, the project was too attractive. Men and women of all classes, even children, started on the crusade. Occasionally some were restrained by the wisdom of their clerical advisers.

All who went on the crusade were to receive plenary indulgence or full remission of sins. This is clear from the canon of the Council, from the statement of Pope Eugene III., and from the letters of Urban to the princes of Flanders and to the people of Bologna. It was reported in various forms by the contemporaries. Fulcher limits it to those who died on the expedition; Robert applies it to all who went. Baldric inserts a rather indefinite statement concerning it in Urban's address to the clergy. Guibert does not mention it in his account of the speech. William applies it to all. It is interesting to compare with these brief statements the very careful exposition of William of Tyre.

Expressions of contempt for the Turks. The terms used by Fulcher, Robert, and Baldric are commonplace enough. . . . William of Malmesbury, on the other hand, has a long passage describing the cowardice and degeneracy of the Turks. His account accords with the general belief of the times. If Urban used contemptuous expressions it would probably have been so much in agreement with their own ideas that his hearers would have paid little heed to this portion of his address. The crusaders were surprised at the bravery of the Turks when they met the latter in battle.

Fight righteous wars instead of the iniquitous combats in which you have been engaged. Mentioned at some length by all.

Promise of eternal rewards. Mentioned by all.

Promise of temporal rewards. Indefinite in Fulcher, but not in Robert or in Baldric. Guibert and William of Malmesbury have no parallel passages, but the same idea of the acquisition of the enemy's country is assumed.

The participants are not to let anything hinder them. Fulcher barely mentions this. Robert gives a much fuller statement, that they are not to be hindered by ties of affection or care for property. Baldric has a passage of the same import. Guibert has no mention of this, but William dwells upon it.

Time of departure. Mentioned only by Fulcher. It seems probable that this was not mentioned in the exhortation but was fixed later. The time actually set for the departure was August 15, 1096.

God will be your leader. Mentioned by Fulcher . . . as the last point in the pope's exhortation. Robert does not have this, but he may have had it in mind when he gave as the concluding sentence of the pope's second address to the clergy, "He that taketh not his cross and followeth after me is not worthy of me." . . .

Praise of the Franks. Robert begins his version with a reference to the Franks as the chosen people beloved by God. His statement does not carry very great weight because this is a favorite thought of his. While a natural beginning under ordinary circumstances, it may not have seemed appropriate after the references to the evil conduct of the people in the previous address. This may have caused Fulcher and Baldric to omit it even if it was a part of the pope's speech. Guibert has no mention of it in the speech, but uses similar language in a preceding chapter. . . .

Special sanctity of Jerusalem. Mentioned by Robert, Baldric, and Guibert at great length. The Holy Sepulchre, in particular, and its profanation are cited. *Evil conditions at home.* Mentioned by all but Fulcher. The latter may have omitted it because he had already given the pope's first speech, in which the evil conditions were discussed at length. *Sufferings of the pilgrims.* Mentioned by Baldric and at great length by Guibert. *The task will be easy.* Mentioned slightly by Baldric, and by William. *Necessity of contending against Antichrist.* This is mentioned only by Guibert. His argument is interesting. It may be summarized baldly: The coming of Antichrist is at hand. According to the prophets he will have his dwelling on the Mount of Olives and will destroy the three Christian kings of Egypt, Africa, and Ethiopia. But these countries are now pagan and there are no Christian kings. Therefore, it is necessary, for the fulfilment of the prophecy, for the Christians to conquer these countries so that there may be Christian kings to be destroyed. Possibly this was Guibert's way of stating the temporal rewards mentioned by the others.

Reference to Spain. Mentioned by William, but by no one else. Guibert, however, does give in the preceding chapter, as one of the causes of the pope's preaching the crusade, that he had very often heard of the Saracens' attack upon Spain. *Cross to be worn.* Mentioned by William. Robert mentions this in the second address to the clergy. The others mention it later but not as a part of the pope's speech.

In addition to the subjects already mentioned there is a subtle appeal to the ascetic spirit of the times, in the versions by Baldric, Guibert, and William; and an exhortation to follow the example of the Old Testament heroes, in the versions by Baldric and Guibert. It is probable that both subjects were referred to by Urban, but the vague and divergent references may be merely the work of the reporters. The references are of too slight weight to be used here.

Urban may have mentioned all these subjects, as well as some which have not been reported. Undoubtedly, his exhortation was much longer than any of the brief reports which have been preserved.

But, judging from the material in existence, the following conclusions seem justified.

In addition to the points about which there can be no reasonable doubt, rich and poor may have been urged to go. If this was not expressly mentioned, it seems to have been taken for granted by the auditors. The evil conditions at home were probably dwelt upon. The only doubt in this case arises from a possible confusion of the first and second speeches in the various reports. Some mention of this subject would, however, naturally accompany the exhortation to fight just wars in place of unjust. The sufferings of the pilgrims were probably mentioned. There may have been some reference to Spain, as this might have been suggested by the conquests of the Turks. The valor of the Franks may have been praised by the Pope. It is a matter of doubt whether Urban used any but commonplace expressions of contempt in describing the Turks or in regard to the easiness of the task. He probably did not refer to the time of departure, to the need of contending against Antichrist, or to the wearing of the cross.

The outline of the pope's speech, therefore, seems to have been as follows:* [Praise of the valor of the Franks]; necessity of aiding the brethren in the East; appeals for aid from the East; victorious advance of the Turks; [reference to Spain]; sufferings of the Christians in the East; (sufferings of the pilgrims); desecration of the churches and holy places; [expressions of contempt concerning the Turks]; special sanctity of Jerusalem; this is God's work; (rich and poor to go); grant of plenary indulgence; fight righteous wars instead of iniquitous combats; (evil conditions at home); promise of eternal and temporal rewards; let nothing hinder you; God will be your leader.

* The subjects concerning which there seems to be no doubt are printed without enclosures; those which the pope probably used are in parentheses, those which he may have used are in brackets; the other subjects are, of course, omitted. The order is determined by a comparison of different versions. [Editor's footnote]

The Crusade and the Eastern Churches

AUGUST C. KREY

August C. Krey was born in Germany in 1887 and came to the United States as a child. He received his higher education at the University of Wisconsin, where he studied under Dana Carleton Munro. After receiving his doctorate at Wisconsin, Krey joined the faculty of the University of Minnesota, where he remained for the rest of his scholarly career. He died in 1961.

THE success of the First Crusade in its capture of Jerusalem and in the foundation of the Latin states in Syria was so unprecedented and so stirring that historians generally have overlooked the possibility that from the point of view of Urban II, who inspired the Crusade, it may have fallen far short of the goal which he hoped to attain when he set it in motion. It is this possibility which the present paper seeks to explore.

In recent years, it is true, there has been an ever widening awareness of the fact that Pope Urban may have sought by way of that Crusade to bring about a union between the Greek and Latin churches. . . .

A number of . . . scholars . . . have reached this conclusion through a variety of shrewd conjectures that, since the material considerations in the agreement [of the Crusaders] with Alexius [Comnenus, the Byzantine Emperor] were so heavily in favor of the latter, there must have been certain less tangible considerations, such as the union of the two churches, perhaps, to establish the balance. Others . . . have arrived at a similar inference through a systematic examination of the previous relations of the churches; and both of these approaches have served to throw new light on the whole discussion. But in striving to weigh and canvass the full extent of the problem more thoroughly, one must also take into account a number of other factors which are to be found in the intricate interplay during the Crusade of all the separate elements which these researches imply.

Some inkling, for instance, of Pope Urban's desire to bring about the union of Greek and Latin Christendom is furnished by the reports of his speech at Clermont. Yet, since none of these was written at the time and since all, furthermore, were naturally influenced by later events, Urban's ambition to achieve this result is much more clearly indicated in the letters which he addressed to the assembling Crusaders. In these he assigned great prominence to the plight of *ecclesias Dei in Orientis partibus* [the churches of God in the eastern regions]; and since he chose, in addition, to single out the liberation of *orientalium ecclesiarum* [the eastern churches] as the major objective of the expedition, one may reasonably assume that his identification of the "oriental churches" as "Churches of God" was no mere casual statement. Rather, it may quite well have been deliberate and, as such, intended to stress the fact that he proposed to make no distinction between Greek and Latin Christians but to regard them all, instead, as common members of one fold, of which the pope at Rome was the proper shepherd.

From August C. Krey, "Urban's Crusade — Success or Failure," in *The American Historical Review*, LIII (January, 1948), pp. 235–250. Reprinted with permission of the American Historical Association.

Other items of evidence to this effect may likewise be drawn from the fact that Urban had already established a record of friendly relations with Emperor Alexius long before Clermont. Furthermore, part of the correspondence of the emperor with the abbot of Monte Cassino has survived, and its tone is also one of friendly co-operation. More significant, perhaps, was the action of Urban in sending military aid, however small, in response to the emperor's request in 1092. This action, as well as the presence of the envoys of Alexius at the Council of Piacenza, about which we know too little, must be counted as important evidence in establishing the probability of some friendly understanding between Urban and Alexius before the First Crusade.

More convincing, though still inferential, are the deductions to be drawn from the conduct of the pope's personal representative or representatives on the expedition itself. These were, in the first instance, Bishop Adhemar of Puy and, secondly, Count Raymond of Toulouse, who was present at Clermont; and it may be safely assumed that Urban discussed his hopes and plans with Adhemar, and possibly also with Count Raymond. Inasmuch as Adhemar accompanied the count's forces on the long journey to the Holy Land, that military leader must likewise have become acquainted with the pope's plans from the bishop, if not from the pope himself.

The first important occasion for the revelation of any previous understanding between pope and emperor was in connection with the treaty which the several leaders of the expedition were required to make with Alexius. This included the agreement between them that all cities and territories which had been previously held by the empire were to be returned to Alexius; and, though no definite date for the earlier boundaries of the empire was specified, Antioch and its environs were apparently included. This fact in itself is enough to make one wonder whether so substantial a concession did not depend on other considerations which may, in turn, have rested

upon some previous understanding with the real leader of the Crusade, Pope Urban. For over a year and a half, at any rate, this agreement was faithfully respected by the crusaders.

In further support of this general thesis, let us return, for the moment, to Urban in Italy, where continued effort on his part was required to persuade the Italians to respond to his call for a crusade. Finally, however, he was successful, enlisting not only southern Normans but the maritime cities, Genoa, Pisa, and Venice, and, last of all, the Lombard region, whose largest contingents started after his death. More significant for our immediate argument, however, is the fact that he carefully planned a church council at Bari to consider the union of Greek and Latin churches. This council, in which the momentarily exiled Anselm, Archbishop of Canterbury, played such an important part, met in October, 1098; and though it is not certain that any of the prelates from Constantinople were present, it adjourned to meet again in Rome the following spring for further consideration of the union of the two churches.

Turning again at this point to the crusading army, and especially to its protracted siege of Antioch, it is clear that, since much of the territory which had been recovered from the Muslim was garrisoned by crusaders, the policy which was adopted in filling church offices in these regions required careful consideration, and the decisions bear on our problem. This becomes evident as soon as one recalls that whenever a former Greek prelate was available he was reinstated. In no instance up to the death of Adhemar were the two churches provided with separate leadership in the same area. So harmonious, indeed, was the relationship at that time between the Greek and Latin churches that Simeon, the Greek patriarch of Jerusalem, who was then a refugee in Cyprus, joined Adhemar in a letter to the West asking for reinforcements. Again, when Antioch was finally secured by the crusaders, Adhemar, who seems to have assumed that the two churches were to be united, arranged for the ceremonial restoration of the Greek patriarch there; and in following this policy there is little reason to doubt that he was faithfully carrying out the instructions of Pope Urban. It fact, the entire consistency of his actions with both the words and the deeds of the pope would seem to indicate that their common understanding must have been based upon something more definite than a vague hope that the union of the two churches might result from the Crusade.

Assuming for the moment, then, that some such agreement between pope and emperor did exist, or at least that the union of the Greek and Latin churches was a definite part of Urban's plan for the Crusade, why do we not hear more about it later? The answer to this question must be sought first of all, the evidence suggests, in the events around and about Antioch, and particularly in those which occurred after the death of Adhemar; and to go very far on this line of inquiry, it is important to remember that Bohemond's desire to keep Antioch for himself was already plain, even before the bishop's death. Moreover, it is Bohemond's own chronicler who assures us most clearly of all that the other leaders, presumably Adhemar among them, did not agree with Bohemond's ambition but, on the contrary, considered Antioch as part of the territory to be returned to Alexius. This disposition on their part is clearly confirmed by the anonymous author of the *Gesta* who reports that, after the final capture of Antioch, the council of leaders sent an embassy, of which Hugh the Great was chief, to Alexius inviting him *"ad recipiendam civitatem"* [to recover the city] and to the fulfillment of his treaty obligations.

So specific a statement can hardly be disregarded; and it is clear from it that, to acquire legal title to Antioch, Bohemond would have to bolster his claim by some more persuasive argument than mere possession. To do so, of course, his most obvious strategy was to discredit the emperor's fulfillment of his treaty obligations; and, if we are to believe Anna [Comnena, daughter of the Byzantine Emperor,] the wily Bohemond was already engaged upon this policy even before Antioch was first entered. No doubt he was, as is further suggested not only by his treatment of Taticius, the military representative of Alexius, but also by his insinuations as to the motives for the latter's departure from the siege of Antioch. Nevertheless, it would be difficult to maintain the thesis that Alexius had failed to live up to his treaty obligations at this time, for he was personally leading an army to aid in the capture of Antioch in 1098 and was well across Asia Minor when he was dissuaded from his purpose by the panic-stricken Stephen of Blois, who assured him that the crusading army had already been destroyed. Upon hearing that report, the energies of the emperor's expedition were accordingly spent in applying the "parched earth" treatment to cover its retreat; and when Hugh finally arrived at the imperial court it was too late for Alexius to launch a new expedition immediately. But he did prepare another for the next year, and his envoys announcing the coming of this expedition reached Antioch as early as February and the main army of the crusaders at Arka by April. In addition, Alexius must also be given credit for the supplies which came by ship from Cyprus and even from Constantinople throughout this period.

How soon Alexius became convinced that the agreement concerning Antioch was to be repudiated is uncertain, for, though Bohemond's intentions in the matter must have become increasingly clear before the year 1098 had run its course, the letter in which they are stated specifically, along with a report of Adhemar's death, was not sent before September 11. This letter from the crusading chieftains to Urban was edited or supplemented by Bohemond when most of the other leaders were absent from Antioch; and in it the pope was urged "now that his vicar was dead, to come in person and establish his see at Antioch 'the original see of Peter himself' — *'urbem principalem et capitalem Christiani nominis.* [the chief and capital city of the name, Christian]'" Writing in the first person, Bohemond assures the pope that he feels quite competent to cope with the Infidel but that the heretics (Greeks, Armenians, Syrians, and Jacobites are specified) are beyond him. To deal with them, he needs the pope's help *"omnes haereses, cuiuscumque generis sint, tua auctoritate et nostra virtute eradicas et destruas* [With your authority and our strength, you may root out and destroy all the heresies, of whatever kind they may be]"; and there in those few words he announces not only his determination to hold Antioch, even though it may mean war with the Greeks to do so, but his not too subtle purpose, furthermore, to gain sanction for his usurpation, at least in the eyes of the Latins, by having the pope establish his see in that city. By 1098, therefore, Bohemond was embarked upon a course that was certain to lead to a war with Alexius for the possession of Antioch, a struggle which was to engage his energies for the rest of his life.

Bohemond's intentions and policy now being clear, it became necessary to discover their effect on (1) the pope, (2) Alexius, and (3) the crusading leaders.

To begin, then, with Urban: How startled he must have been, if our conjecture about his hopes and his plans is correct, to receive the letter of September 11, which, though written ostensibly by all the crusading leaders, ended so clearly as a personal appeal from Bohemond alone. And indeed he had reason to be surprised by its whole general tenor, for he was not accustomed to thinking of Greek Christians as 'heretics' nor had his representative, Adhemar, ever treated the Greek clergy as such; and as he pondered over the letter in question, it must have been very soon clear to him that he had hardly to read between its lines to gather that Bohemond was at least contemplating, if

not already set upon, a course which could only lead, if carried out, to a complete reversal of the policies which had hitherto been followed.

Just when Urban received this portentous communication we do not know; for ships and fleets traveled with so little speed in those years that there are instances during the early twelfth century when certain important messages from Syria to Italy were as long in transit as all of six months. So it is doubtful whether this special letter could have reached any Italian port much before the end of the year; and even after it arrived there, it had still to be carried to its final destination.

As uncertain, therefore, as we must remain about the date of its arrival, we are no more sure as to what its immediate effect upon Urban may have been. From the nature of its contents, however, one might suppose that no hasty reply was likely to be sent. For, as the pope thought over the information which was thus conveyed to him, he could hardly have failed to understand that its import was such as to represent considerably more than a passing threat to the forthcoming council at Rome, where the question of unity with the Greek church, which had already been debated at Bari in the previous fall, was again to receive major attention. As to how soon that was clear to him, we can only speculate, of course; but the very fact that the reports of this council contain almost no mention of the chief question which it was supposed to consider might lead one to infer that Bohemond's letter had been so disturbing to both pope and Greeks alike as to render further discussion of unity momentarily impossible.

Some new course of action was obviously required; but on what Urban decided or, indeed, whether he ever reached a conclusion on this matter is not at all clear, for he lived little more than three months after the Council of Rome, and he may have been ill most of this time. It has usually been assumed, however, that Daimbert or Dagobert, Archbishop of Pisa, was sent by him to succeed Adhemar as the papal representative on the Crusade. But this is pure assumption. All the chronological indexes that we possess indicate that Daimbert and his Pisan fleet were already at sea long before Urban received or could have received the official notification of Adhemar's death. At most, Daimbert went as ecclesiastical leader of the Pisan contribution to the Crusade, which he had done so much to enlist. True, he was the ranking Latin prelate in the East when he arrived, and therefore assumed a position of ecclesiastical leadership, but that is another story. For our immediate purposes, it is important only to remember that he was not Urban's appointee to succeed Adhemar. It is doubtful, in fact, whether Urban ever nominated a successor; and there is reason to believe that Cardinal Maurice, who was appointed by Paschal II in April, 1100, was the first papal vicar after Adhemar. If so, every crucial event of the Crusade from August 1, 1098, until the arrival of Cardinal Maurice, must have occurred without the presence or the guidance of any official representative of the pope. And, if we accept this view, we may therefore conclude not only that Bohemond's letter quite probably served to paralyze the efforts of Urban II to push forward his plans for unifying the Greek and Latin churches but also that the pope himself died before he was able to go any further with that hope or expectation.

As to what may have been the effect of Bohemond's actions on Alexius, whatever disquieting rumors may have reached the emperor by the time Hugh the Great arrived at Constantinople toward the end of July, 1098, they must have been more than offset by the reports of that official messenger, for Alexius immediately began preparations for another expedition, and he furthermore sent envoys to the crusaders to announce its coming. These envoys reached Antioch in February, 1099; and then and there only did they learn for certain that Bohemond meant to keep that city. Nor did they know until they moved

on to Arka in April that the crusading army meant to go on to Jerusalem without waiting for the forces of the emperor. As a consequence, the expedition which Alexius had prepared to aid the Crusade was diverted into an attack upon Antioch and the region thereabout. Thus unexpectedly, at least on the part of Alexius, was the war between him and Bohemond begun; and until that should be settled, the emperor was hardly in a mood to co-operate in any plan looking toward unity between the two churches.

Having considered the effect of Bohemond's policy upon Pope Urban and Emperor Alexius, we must also try to estimate its impact on the rest of the crusading leaders. To proceed with that inquiry, then, it is highly important to recall not only the fact that the council of crusading leaders had sent Hugh the Great to urge Alexius to come to receive Antioch and fulfill his obligations to the crusaders but also, in addition, that this action was taken *after* the capture of that city in 1098 and likewise after Bohemond had won, it is thought, the promise of the majority of the leaders to give him possession of it. Furthermore, Hugh had been sent on his mission before the death of Adhemar; and, to judge from all this whole series of events, one can only conclude that, on sober second thought and after the crisis at Antioch was past, the crusaders' leaders must have repented of their earlier action in promising Bohemond the city which was so manifestly due Alexius under terms of their agreement with him. Doubtless it was Adhemar's influence which thus prevailed; but whatever may have moved them to this decision, their attitude at the end of June or early in July, 1098, was based apparently, as officially voiced, on the understanding that even if any considerable number of them had made concessions to Bohemond about Antioch before its capture, their previous agreement with Alexius was bound to supersede any or all such commitments to Bohemond. Whether this general decision of the council also implied that, if Alexius failed to live up to his full contract with the crusading leaders, they would then approve Bohemond's claim to Antioch, is not certain.

After the death of Adhemar, Count Raymond of Toulouse became the leader of the opposition to Bohemond's plans, and much of the bickering that went on among the crusading leaders during the fall and winter of 1098–1099 was concerned, in general, with the disposition of Antioch. Though there were many other questions that came up during that time, this was the most persistent and far-reaching, so much so, indeed, that when the decision to march on Jerusalem was finally made, Bohemond seems to have given a somewhat equivocal promise to participate. At any rate, he apparently accompanied the rest for only a short distance southward, and then returned to Antioch in a withdrawal which Raymond, who felt himself too far committed to abandon the march, vigorously resented.

The next test of the opinion of the crusading leaders came in April, 1099, at Arka, near Tripoli, where the envoys of Alexius, after their fruitless stay in Antioch, reached the main crusading army and urged the crusaders to await the coming of Alexius and his expedition, which was promised on St. John's Day. Count Raymond strongly urged that course also, and the decision of the leaders to reject this advice was compounded of so many diverse interests that it can scarcely be regarded as a clear indication of their attitude toward either Bohemond or Alexius. For the rank and file were impatient and anxious to complete their vows; and since Raymond had indicated a deep interest, which aroused no enthusiasm among the other leaders, in capturing Tripoli for himself, his motives in counseling delay were questioned even by his own followers, thus losing the position of leadership which he had held since Bohemond abandoned the march toward Jerusalem. His wishes, and possibly his hopes, regarding the disposition of the Holy City were thwarted by the other leaders, of whom Robert of Normandy was his leading opponent at Jerusalem, as he had been at Arka earlier.

In the light of these developments, the incidents at Laodicea, where the homebound crusaders encountered Bohemond, may seem strange, for there both Robert of Normandy and Robert of Flanders sided with Raymond when he took an active stand against Bohemond, who was energetically engaged in the siege of that Greek town. In this effort Bohemond had won the aid of Archbishop Daimbert and his recently arrived Pisan fleet. With this help the capture of the city was assured; and, under the circumstances, it is hardly surprising that his old rival, Raymond of Toulouse, expressed strong opposition to Bohemond's plans. Yet even if Raymond's position can be thus accounted for, that of the two Roberts is far from clear, for there is every reason to believe that they personally preferred Bohemond. That they nevertheless joined Raymond in the threat to take up arms against Bohemond, unless he desisted from the siege, can best be accounted for on the assumption that his opposition reflected not only his own interests but also the original plan of Urban as executed by Adhemar up to the latter's death. In such a situation, of course, the two Roberts could do no less than acknowledge, as they had done in the council of leaders in Antioch after Karbuqa's defeat, the justice of Raymond's contention; for Bohemond's action at Laodicea, which was included in the environs of Antioch, had again brought into sharp focus the whole question of the return of that city to Alexius. As a result of so many combined protests, Archbishop Daimbert called off his Pisan fleet, and devoted his energies to reconciling the Latin leaders, while Bohemond was forced to give up the siege. In spite of that, however, and even though the two Roberts returned to the West with their troops, Raymond and a considerable portion of his troops remained in or near Laodicea to assure protection of the Greek city; and when he himself finally sailed to Constantinople to confer with Alexius, he left his family and his troops behind. Looking closely, therefore, at this whole episode, one is led to conclude that Raymond and the two Roberts must have regarded Bohemond's conduct at Laodicea as a violation not only of their common agreement with Alexius but also of the plans of Pope Urban. In addition, the circumstances would seem also to imply that Daimbert could hardly have been Urban's appointee to succeed Adhemar.

And now to go a step further in the thesis which is here being advanced, let us turn our attention more directly on the war between Bohemond and Alexius. The troops of Alexius had been operating about the periphery of Antioch in the summer and early fall of 1099, but military operations had ceased at the approach of winter. The respite which the unfavorable season offered made it possible for Bohemond to fulfill his crusader's vow by going to Jerusalem for Christmas; and on this pious excursion he was joined by Archbishop Daimbert, who had spent the better part of the fall in flitting between the troops of Raymond at Laodicea and those of Bohemond at Antioch. These two ambitious men, Bohemond and Daimbert, were thus able to perfect their plans; and when they arrived at Jerusalem it was Bohemond who engineered the project for the deposition of Arnulf as patriarch of Jerusalem and the elevation of Daimbert to that office. It was also Bohemond who, when this had been accomplished, arranged for the joint submission of Godfrey and himself as vassals for their respective principalities to Patriarch Daimbert. This was no boon to Godfrey, but it was to Bohemond, who hoped thereby to commit the Latin church to the full support of his claim to Antioch, which neither the crusading leaders nor Alexius had recognized; and the fact that this ambition on his part was involved in his dealings with Daimbert is amply confirmed by the much-disputed letter of Daimbert to Bohemond, which the troops of Raymond intercepted and William of

Tyre published. Neither of these schemers profited too much, it is true, from this transaction, for Bohemond was captured by the Turks in 1101, and the new papal legate, Robert, who arrived at Jerusalem in 1102, deposed Daimbert, who then sought refuge in Antioch, where he remained until Bohemond was released from captivity and decided to return to the West for reinforcements.

It was doubtless before or on that westward journey that the further plans of these two were perfected. Embracing not only Bohemond's plans for a new crusade and Daimbert's desire to recover the patriarchate of Jerusalem, they may also have included the decision to spread abroad a much edited revision of the anonymous *Gesta Francorum* [The Deeds of the Franks] as propaganda material for Bohemond's primary design. Whatever these conspirators may have had in mind, their plans received a very favorable reception in Rome in 1105 at the hands of Paschal II, who had succeeded Urban as pope; and the end result of their efforts was that Daimbert was reinstated, and Bohemond was given the help of a papal legate in his new appeal for a new crusade, especially in France. This change in papal attitude need not, however, concern us at the moment, for the war between Alexius and Bohemond had altered any prospect of a union between the Greek and Latin churches until the question of Antioch was settled.

Turning once more to Alexius, then, we find that monarch intent, from the year 1099, upon the recovery of Antioch; and in this private war of his own, Bohemond's enemies were his friends — a circumstance which must have caused him no little embarrassment in dealing with the Crusade of 1101. For Bohemond's enemies, then, including the Turks who lived near Antioch, were now Alexius' friends. Thus Alexius was asked to help the crusaders (many of whom would doubtless turn against him when they discovered that he was at war with the Latins of Antioch) against the Turks who were his allies in that war. It was a difficult spot to be in, so difficult, in fact, that the disasters which befell the Crusade of 1101 in its march across Asia Minor were in part blamed upon Alexius. When Bohemond was released from captivity and resumed active leadership of the war against Alexius, he found the alliance of the latter with the Turks too strong for his limited forces. It was this fact which led him to seek additional aid from the West. Alexius suspected his design and began recruiting a strong army with which to meet Bohemond in the West, and Arabic chroniclers inform us that he had no difficulty in recruiting Muslim troops for this purpose.

As Alexius had correctly surmised, Bohemond landed his "Crusade" of 1107 in the neighborhood of Durazzo, and it was there that Alexius had concentrated his greatest efforts in meeting the threat. To repel it and to defeat Bohemond, he used persuasion, bribery, and force, and Bohemond was forced at last to an ignominious peace. What interests us most about the terms which were then drawn up between him and Alexius is the fact that he, Bohemond, was not only required by it to recognize the previous agreement of 1097 but also to reinstate in Antioch a single Greek patriarch, who was to be nominated by Alexius. This provision, which implies that Alexius, too, had accepted the idea of a unified church, recalls the action of Urban's representative, Adhemar, in setting up a former Greek patriarch in Antioch as the sole ecclesiastical head of that city. That nothing came of this treaty is beside the point, for the greatest efforts of Alexius against Bohemond in the West had made it impossible for him to exert anything like an equal amount of pressure in the East; and, as a natural consequence of that fact, Tancred was able to hold out so successfully that Antioch remained an independent principality of the Latins until the time of Manuel, grandson of Alexius. But when it became at last a fief of Manuel, the discussions of the union of Greek and Latin churches were again resumed with some prospect of success.

That, however, is to anticipate events; and we are concerned here only with the fact that when the treaty was signed and Bohemond's hostile forces had left the Balkan peninsula, Alexius seems to have felt a sense of great relief, as well he might since Bohemond's career was virtually ended. Though the latter returned to Italy and started to raise another army, he had made little progress in that endeavor when illness and death overtook him March 7, 1111. No doubt the news of his death afforded Alexius even greater assurance, and we soon find him reopening negotiations with the pope that involved specific reference to the reunion of Greek and Latin churches. As evidence that the initiative came from the emperor, one has only to read the letter of Paschal II to Alexius in 1112; and the longer one meditates on that letter the more one is tempted to reflect that the overtures which Alexius put forward at that time may have been but a repetition of those which his envoys had conveyed to Urban II at Piacenza in 1094 or even earlier and which may, therefore, have constituted the basis of Urban's great hopes and plans for the First Crusade.

If the pope's instructions had been more fully carried out, it is easy to see now, the prospect of that union between the Greek and Latin churches would have come much nearer fulfillment; but that great opportunity was lost, or rather defeated, by the unbridled ambition of one man, Bohemond, who seemed to carry that strain in his blood. For poets and novelists might find an abundance of material in the remarkable similarity of the roles which he and his father, Robert Guiscard, both played in two papal efforts to unify the two great branches of the Christian church. Such unity, indeed, had been one of the dearest wishes of Gregory VII; and though circumstances prevented his launching a crusade, yet the prospect of the union apparently never left his mind — a fact which Guiscard was canny enough to recognize and make use of in furthering his own attempts to gain support for his attack on the Greek Empire. And, as events turned out, Gregory was thus forced into a position where he seemed to be trying to attain by force what could only have been attained through persuasion and co-operation. In the same way, also, Bohemond strove in his turn to commit Urban to a program of force which he virtually succeeded in winning from Urban's successor; and as an end result of this double scheming of father and son, the two popes who might otherwise have succeeded in bringing about the much-sought union between the two churches were both thwarted in their purposes.

Taking into consideration, then, all the factors which bear on the question we have been surveying, it would seem that, however much Urban desired the other objectives of the Crusade, his chief aim was to bring about the union of the Greek and Latin churches under the headship of the bishop of Rome; and this conclusion, which forms the thesis of this paper, is not inconsistent apparently with the course of church history. For too much has been made of the so-called "definitive break" between the Greek and Latin churches in 1054, and too little of the efforts that were made during the great reform movement of the eleventh century to achieve uniformity of Christian doctrine and practice. As a matter of fact, there was nothing definite about the affair of 1054, for negotiations for union and for the elimination of variant practices in the two churches were resumed from time to time after that date, and the initiation of such negotiations were undertaken by Greeks as well as Latins. Furthermore, such negotiations have recurred through the centuries right down to the present.

The most remarkable feature of the affair of 1054, it seems in retrospect, was the uncompromising insistence of the Latin church that the union or reunion of Greek and Latin churches must be under the headship of the pope at Rome; and this change of emphasis, it would also seem,

must have developed as a logical consequence of the great Western church reform program. This movement, which nearly all textbooks on medieval history describe as devoted to the elimination of simony, marriage of the clergy, and lay investiture, also supplied, in addition, as is seldom recognized, the over-all drive to re-establish uniformity of church service and practice, and even of dogma, which had seriously disintegrated under the effects of early feudalism. That this drive for so much reform came from north of the Alps, not from Italy, and that its core was consistently monastic, seems — again on the long view — important; for the north, unlike Italy, was scarcely conscious of any Greek influence, nor did it share any tradition of occasional submission to Constantinople. On the contrary, the people of that region were conscious only of the fact that their religion had come from Rome; and the monastic core of the reformers' drive explains its uncompromising attitude on the fundamentals of ecclesiastical uniformity. Furthermore, the congregation of Cluny, which in a sense epitomizes the whole movement, supplied a sustained nucleus for its propagation; and whether we date the beginning of the movement in 910 or at some later time in eastern France or southern and western Germany, the reform drive had still gained such momentum that its force was effectively felt in nearly every portion of Western Christendom before it captured Rome in 1046.

After that time, the identification of the popes with the leadership of that great reform movement inspired them with a consciousness of strength and a confidence born of a long succession of victories over many obstinate difficulties; for though they were now confronted with the practical problem of dealing with Greek churches in southern Italy, they had already met and overcome a variety of other troublesome differences. So when Leo IX addressed himself to that specific problem, he was able to do so in the very same spirit which had served to iron out other such difficulties in the North and West. When viewed in this light, therefore, the affair of 1054 meant merely that Constantinople was gaining at that time its first acquaintance with this new revival in the Latin church, and that that experience proved momentarily to be nothing less than breath-taking.

In general, this confident attitude continued in the papacy, and men of Cluny were there to sustain it throughout the rest of the eleventh century. Abbot Hugh, for example, who became head of Cluny in 1048, was still abbot in 1109, having lived to see at least two of the monks whom he had trained become popes. He was abbot when Leo IX took up the Greek problem, was with Gregory at Canossa, and counseled Urban before the memorable meeting at Clermont; and doubtless he too was fired on all these occasions by the dream of Urban that all Christendom might be united. Doubtless, also, he shared Urban's disappointment that the Crusade had failed to realize that dream, for from Urban's point of view the Crusade that he planned could hardly have been counted a complete success.

The Pope's Plan for the Crusade

FREDERIC DUNCALF

Frederic Duncalf, who was, like A. C. Krey, a student under Dana Carleton Munro at the University of Wisconsin, was born in 1882. After taking his doctorate, Duncalf taught at Bowdoin College, the University of Illinois, and, for the major part of his career, at the University of Texas. In addition to several articles which appeared in the *American Historical Review*, Professor Duncalf was instrumental in organizing the participation of numerous scholars in writing the co-operative five-volume *History of the Crusades* which is in process of being published by the University of Pennsylvania. Duncalf himself contributed two chapters to the first volume of this project. He died in 1963.

URBAN II, who started the proposed First Crusade, had a plan for carrying through his great project. In a general way it is possible to reconstruct the original papal program for the crusade. Urban issued definite instructions, a few of which have been preserved. He also indicated quite clearly what the aims and policy of the crusaders should be. What influence did these ideas have upon the course of events which resulted in the restoration of much of Asia Minor to the Byzantine Empire, and the establishment of Latin colonies in the East? There are suggestions that the pope impressed the essential points of his plan for the crusade so deeply on the minds of the leaders that they long hesitated to deviate from such instructions. If this view is tenable, it offers a reasonable interpretation of many of the puzzling events of the crusade.

The pope first gave unity to his undertaking by formulating definite and precise aims. The heterogenous host, headed by many lords who had little training for such a coöperative enterprise, needed the unifying influence of a clear-cut purpose, for which there was a deep and lasting religious enthusiasm. The real objective of the crusade, as it is indicated in the letters and reported speeches of the pope, was the Holy Land. The birthplace of Christianity was to be recovered and preserved from the defiling hands of the Infidels. This was the idea which fired enthusiasm throughout the West, and put real vigor into the crusading movement. Furthermore, the crusaders were bound to fulfill this pilgrimage to Jerusalem by vows, which were pledges not lightly to be broken. The church could make deserters return to the East to complete the journey which they had sworn to carry through. The crusaders could not forget that their destination was the Holy Land. However, before this conception of uniting western Christendom in an effort to rescue the Holy Sepulchre took form, Urban II, and Gregory VII before him, had considered the possibility of sending aid to the eastern empire. This idea was incorporated in the crusade and became its secondary purpose. The pope sought to arouse sympathy for the eastern Christians, who were oppressed by the Turks, and urged the people of the West to go to their assistance as a religious duty. It is possible that he hoped the crusade would promote better feeling between the East and the West, and that this could further the movement for the reunion of the Greek and

Roman churches, in which he was interested. This question of union had been the subject of negotiation between pope and emperor, and Alexius had proposed that a council be held at Constantinople to discuss the matter. The pope, then, gave the crusade two aims: the recovery of the Holy Land, and the deliverance of the eastern Christians.

The men who so enthusiastically undertook these tasks also accepted his plan for accomplishing them. Urban had no intention of entrusting his armies to divine guidance, although he proclaimed that the Lord would be their leader. Such information as we have indicates that he directed the organization of the crusading movement, and had a policy which he expected would be followed. He knew that someone was needed to keep harmony among the various lay lords, and, unable to go in person, he gave the crusaders an ecclesiastical commander, Bishop Adhemar of Puy, whose appointment was announced at Clermont. There can be no doubt about the role of leadership which he intended this papal legate to play, for he specifically said that the crusaders were to obey him in all things. It may be assumed that Adhemar was fully informed about the pope's plan for the expedition. Urban also set a date, July 15, 1096, for the final departure of the crusading armies from the West. He did not wish people who were unfit for crusading to go. His instructions specifically eliminated old men, and women without their husbands. Finally, all the armies were to gather at Constantinople to begin the war against the Turks.

The manner in which the march to the East was conducted also suggests that some common policy was followed. The crusaders were not as disorderly as has been commonly assumed. To be sure there were camp followers (*pauperes*), who were unprepared for the journey, but the majority of the crusaders had sufficient means to pay their way. The accounts show that they resorted to foraging only when they were refused markets where they could buy their food. In Byzantine territory, regular arrangements were made for markets, and imperial officials took charge of the provisioning of the armies. Another reason for the march being at least as orderly as could be expected for such armies, was the desire of the crusaders to treat all Christian peoples with consideration. There is every reason to believe that the crusaders went East with no feeling of ill will toward the Greeks, whom the pope had sent them to help. The accounts of the chroniclers are colored with the hatred which developed later, but there are suggestions of what the original attitude of the westerners must have been. Thus Godfrey, Robert of Flanders, and other leaders are reported to have told the count of Toulouse that it would be wrong to fight Christians, although Godfrey, himself, had been willing enough to attack the emperor a short time before. In their calmer moments these hotheaded westerners remembered that they had come to aid the Greeks, who were fellow Christians.

Up to the arrival at Constantinople, it is evident that the crusading leaders followed the pope's plan and not their own. To what extent did the pope's aims and policy influence the crusaders in the negotiation of the treaty which they made with Alexius? Unfortunately, we have no evidence of any papal instructions, and as the papal legate was injured on the way to Constantinople, we do not know that he took part in the discussion of the treaty. However, in view of the fact that the crusade was recognized to be the pope's enterprise, it is reasonable to conjecture that the crusaders were prepared to make arrangements to coöperate with the emperor, whom they were to aid against the Turks. The pope most certainly expected that Alexius would welcome the crusaders. Otherwise, he would hardly have selected Constantinople as the mobilization point for his armies. Urban knew that the basileus wanted military help from the West. Messengers from the emperor had come to the council at Piacenza with such a request. No doubt, Alexius wanted mercenaries, but he did not dream of the great religious movement which the pope would awaken. On the other hand, the pope, once he had decided to preach the crusade, most certainly thought that the crusading armies could give the emperor far more help than a few mercenaries. Urban, who optimistically hoped that Greeks and Latins could again unite in one church, did not foresee the bad feeling which the crusade was to provoke. In his enthusiasm, he planned to send forth armies inspired by his own conception of a religious war against the Infidels in which all Christians, Greek or Latin, could unite. Although he was sending an independent religious expedition and not mercenaries, the pope surely did not think that he would embarrass the emperor in what he was doing.

The emperor asked for aid, and the pope was sending it. Did they communicate with each other? It is reasonable to assume that they did, but we have no proof of such relations. The emperor was certainly informed of the favorable reception of his request at Piacenza, where, according to Bernold, Urban asked "many" to take oaths to aid the emperor. The expectation of such aid should have caused Alexius to seek further information as to when and how it was coming. On the other hand, the pope, who was planning to send the crusaders through the Byzantine empire, should have had foresight enough to inform the emperor that they were coming, and should have been interested in making arrangements for the reception of his armies in the East. One of the western lords did take the precaution to announce his coming to Alexius. There are historical rumors of an exchange of letters, and even of an embassy from the pope to the basileus, but they lack certainty of historical evidence. From the council of Piacenza to the arrival of the crusaders in the Byzantine empire, the relations between the East and the West are veiled in tantalizing obscurity.

In the absence of all knowledge of any previous understanding between the pope and the emperor, we can only conjecture what was the attitude of the crusaders on the one hand and of the emperor on the other. Was the emperor willing to accept the help of the crusaders? No doubt he was surprised at the religious character of the movement as well as by the great number of people who had enlisted in the pope's armies. It is also frequently assumed that he was afraid the crusaders would forget their crusading purpose and become ambitious to conquer his territory. Chalandon, for example, believes that the pope did the emperor a great injustice in sending this horde of westerners into the empire. To be sure, the westerners were troublesome fellows to handle, but it may be doubted if they caused the emperor as much embarrassment as many writers would have us believe. Even if Alexius was badly informed of the character of the crusade, he was surely astute enough to find out quickly from the crusaders themselves that they had come to help him, and that they had no intentions of taking any of his territory. He might have suspected the intentions of his former enemy, Bohemond, and thought that the armies contained other adventurers of the same kind. However, it should have been evident to the emperor that the expedition as a whole was bound for Jerusalem where the crusaders intended to fulfill their vows, and that on the way through Asia Minor they would fight the Turks. If the crusaders, then, pursued the aims which the pope had given them, the emperor had no more to fear from them than an occasional outbreak of western violence. On the other hand, he would profit from the war which the crusaders intended to wage with the Turks. There is no indication that the emperor had any thought of not accepting the aid of the crusade. Did he have the intention of accepting it as the pope intended him to have it? The pope had sent an independent expedition which had as its main purpose the recovery of the Holy Land. If the emperor had tried and succeeded in making mercenaries out of the crusaders, he would have broken up the pope's enterprise.

Alexius seems to have made some effort to do this. He adopted the policy of inviting the leaders to come to Constantinople ahead of their armies so that he could negotiate with them separately. He attempted to influence them by promising them splendid gifts if they would accept the terms which he proposed. One by one, the leaders took an oath to him, and according to the accounts he seems to have had little trouble in coming to terms with most of them. If these original oaths were like the final treaty, the leaders obligated themselves to restore such imperial territory as they might conquer from the Turks, and there is no indication that they were not willing to do this. However, the anonymous author of the *Gesta* indicates that the leaders felt that they were in some way forced to take oaths that were unfair to them, and that they did not swear willingly.

The old count of Toulouse, Raymond, was stubborn, and would not swear to the same oath as that which the other leaders had taken. His reasons for not doing so are suggestive. The others had sworn homage and fealty to Alexius, thereby becoming his vassals, although in what manner we do not know. It is of course possible that the westerners did this because they were familiar with no other form of treaty or contract than that between lord and vassal. However that may be, it is clear that Raymond objected to this implication of vassalage. He said that he had not come to get another lord, or to fight for any other lord than the one for whom he had left his country and his patrimonial possessions. Nevertheless, he was willing to pledge himself, his men, and all his wealth if the emperor would go with an army to Jerusalem. However, the emperor excused himself by saying that he had to stay and defend his empire. The *Gesta* says that Raymond swore to respect the life and honor of the emperor, but when asked to take the oath of homage he declared that he would not do so on peril of his head. Raymond, then, was willing to coöperate with the emperor as an independent ally, but objected to an oath by which he would become a vassal. It may be suggested that the old count, who was closely associated with the papal legate, was following the papal ideas in that he did not intend to be diverted from the main purpose of the crusade.

It may be that Raymond attached too much importance to the oath of homage. On the other hand it may be that his obstinacy forced the other leaders who may have wavered to get in line with him. At any rate, the terms of the treaty show that the crusaders were really allies of the emperor for the war against the Turks in Asia Minor and perhaps for the whole crusade. They pledged themselves to restore to Alexius "whatever lands or cities they captured which had once belonged to the empire, and which were now in the hands of its enemies." In return, the emperor promised "to give military aid to the crusaders on land and sea, and eventually to assume command in person of the Greek forces coöperating with the Franks, to furnish them with markets where they could buy food during the campaign, to make reparation for all losses sustained by the Franks, and to guarantee the safety of all pilgrims passing through the Byzantine Empire." These terms indicate that the crusade was to go on its way as the pope intended. If the emperor had tried to divert the leaders and make mercenaries of them, he had failed. He was forced to accept the aid of the pope in the form in which it had been sent to him. It would seem that Urban's policy triumphed at Constantinople. How much longer did it continue to direct the crusade?

Two factors threatened to break down the force of the original ideas which Urban had held about the crusade. First, the ambition to make conquests for themselves grew in the minds of the leaders as they marched southward, and this produced factions which threatened to break up the unity of the crusade. Although they had left the West without any well defined plans of their own, they now began to formulate individualistic policies. In the second place the attitude of friendliness toward the eastern Christians began to weaken. Greek and Latin were unable to coöperate with each other, because they failed to understand each other's point of view. Nevertheless the crusaders seem to have been faithful to the treaty. As a result of their campaign, the emperor was able to gain possession of much of Asia Minor, and he certainly had little cause to complain of the aid which the pope had sent him. Furthermore, the crusaders seem to have remained friendly to the Greeks, and to have stuck to their general plan until they reached Antioch. When in camp near this city, Anselm of Ribemonte wrote home that the mother western church should rejoice to have produced such sons, who not only had made such names for themselves, but had aided the eastern church in such a wonderful manner. The spirit with which Urban had inspired them was not yet dead.

Although it may be pushing too far what is after all a theory, it may be suggested that Raymond of Toulouse was again the defender of the papal ideas of the crusade at Antioch. Bohemond departed from the papal policy in two ways. He deserted the main expedition in order to secure Antioch for himself, and he also started a campaign of hatred against the Greeks. His argument that Antioch should not be restored to the emperor because the basileus had not kept his pledges to the crusaders, clearly had great weight. Alexius had given the westerners reason to be suspicious of his intentions. Nevertheless, to break with the Greeks meant a departure from the plan of the crusade, and this Raymond and the other leaders did not wish to do. They insisted on giving the emperor a chance to make good, and sent messengers to him asking him to come and take Antioch and fulfill his pledges. Although it may be said that they were trying to thwart Bohemond's ambition because of personal hatred for him, it is nevertheless true that they were loyal to the pope's ideas, and Bohemond was the insurgent.

That this was clearly understood is shown by the letter of April or July 1098, which the leaders wrote to the pope, where an effort was made to explain the change in policy which had taken place in the crusade. After announcing the death of the papal legate, Adhemar, the leaders asked the pope to come over and take charge of his expedition. They had been able to conquer the Turks and the pagans, but they had not been able to overcome the heretics, namely the Greeks, Armenians, Syrians, and Jacobites, and they asked the pope to come and eradicate these peoples. The easterners, including their allies, the Greeks, had ceased to be fellow Christians; instead they were heretics. This letter is supposed to be Bohemond's work and he added a postscript which the other leaders probably did not see, in which he asked the pope to release his sons from their oaths to the unjust emperor who had promised much and done little. This was Norman propaganda. Raymond and the other leaders continued to be friendly to the emperor and did not regard the Greeks in an unfriendly way. Laodicea, which is south of Antioch, was handed over to the Greeks, and when Bohemond later attempted to take it he was driven off by Raymond and the other leaders who were returning from Jerusalem.

Bohemond's example encouraged all the leaders to try to win cities for themselves, and in the end it was the common folk who forced the leaders to relinquish such ambitions, and go on with the main business of the crusade. When this was accomplished by the capture of Jerusalem, and the crusaders had fulfilled their vows, most of them prepared to return home. It became necessary, therefore, to provide for the permanent defense of the Holy City. Can we find any indication of papal policy in the arrangement which was made for this purpose?

The pope seems to have intended to have the crusaders make conquests in the Holy Land. He held out inducements to the western lords by telling them that it was a "land flowing with milk and honey." Some of the leaders accepted the pope's suggestion. Raymond took an oath to spend the rest of his life in the East, and Godfrey disposed of his western holdings. Bohemond, we may be sure, expected to find a better principality than he could hope to acquire in Italy. The pope then and the crusaders had intentions of conquest. Now it is not probable that the pope intended the crusaders to occupy any territories which the Greek emperor might claim legitimately. The readiness of the crusaders to pledge themselves to restore imperial territory suggests that they may have been instructed to do so by the pope. On the other hand, it is reasonable to believe that Urban did intend the westerners to keep the Holy Land, in which he and the people of the West had such religious interest. It may be that Alexius objected to this idea and he could, of course, claim that Syria and Palestine had once been part of the empire. However, if the pope had told the crusaders that they could have the Holy Land, Alexius, in order to get back Asia Minor, had to let them have their way. The treaty evidently drew a line between what was to be restored and what was presumably open to western conquest.

Did the pope plan for a church state in the Holy Land? In the absence of any statement by him, and because it is impossible to find any indication of a recognition of papal plans in what happened at Jerusalem, we cannot say. The papal legate was dead, and although the clerical party attempted to set up a church state, the lay leaders were concerned about providing for the military occupation of what had been conquered. However, Raymond, whom we have found defending what seemed to be the papal plan before, declined the kingship with the cryptic remark that he would not wear a crown of gold where Christ had worn a crown of thorns. Godfrey, furthermore, did not receive the title of king, but was made advocate or Defender of the Holy Sepulchre. Later, when Daimbert, the papal legate, became patriarch of Jerusalem, Godfrey and Bohemond received title to their possessions from him. Perhaps there is a suggestion in all this that the crusaders were still showing regard for what they knew the pope wanted. If so, the policy of Urban had influence with them to the very end of the crusade. It would seem that amid all the changing circumstances through which the crusaders passed they did not depart from what they knew were the intentions of the pope without great hesitation. If some of them forgot the spirit and aims of the undertaking, the others recalled them to the task which the pope had given them. They were self-seeking and ambitious enough, it is true, but is it not a safe premise to assume that their medieval religious consciences never allowed them to disregard entirely the aims and plan which the pope had made them vow to fulfill?

The Recovery of the Holy Land

LOUIS BRÉHIER

Louis Bréhier, born in 1868, was a distinguished French medievalist who devoted much of his long scholarly career to the study of Byzantine history and art. His book on the Crusades, *L'Église et l'Orient au moyen âge: Les Croisades* has long been an influential interpretative study of the movement and is still one of the best introductions to Crusade history.

IN 1064 the Seljuks, masters of the Caliphate of Baghdad, began to threaten the unbroken frontiers of the Byzantine Empire. At first they attacked its dependencies. Ani, the principal city of Byzantine Armenia, fell into their hands (July 6, 1064) and they were able to extend their ravages up to the Euphrates. The Armenian prince of Kars, unable to defend himself, gave his state up to the Empire and received in exchange a territory in the Cilician Tarsus. This was the origin of Little Armenia. In 1068 Alp Arslan, the nephew and successor of [the Turkish leader] Tughrul-Beg, crossed the Euphrates and seized Caesarea in Cappadocia, one of the great ecclesiastical metropolises of the Empire. The barbarians pillaged the Church of St. Basil and profaned the saint's tomb. At the same time the Turks were attacking the possessions of the Fatimids. The Khwarismian, Atziz ibn Abik, took Jerusalem in 1070 and massacred three thousand Muslims, although he spared the Christians, who were protected by the walls of their quarter. One of Constantinople's best generals, Romanus Diogenes, was proclaimed emperor in 1067 and attempted to stop the invasion by a major effort. But his magnificent army of 100,000 men (one division of which was commanded by a Frenchman, Roussel de Bailleul) was completely destroyed at the Battle of Manzikert. Romanus himself was taken prisoner and Asia Minor was left open without defence to invasion (1071). Asia Minor became the Sultanate of Rūm, with its capital at Iconium, while one of Alp Arslan's sons seized Jerusalem (1078). The Turks were soon masters of the entire East. Their emirs were established at Nicaea and at Cyzicus in 1081. In 1084 the great city of Antioch, which had been Christian once again since the time of Nicephorus Phocas [963–69], was taken. In 1092 the Turks penetrated to Smyrna, Clazomenae, Chios, Lesbos, Samos, and Rhodes. One by one the asiatic cities, distinguished by memories of the apostolic age or of the doctors of the church, fell into Muslim hands.

The westerners could not remain indifferent to this catastrophe which threatened to lay low the Byzantine Empire and which marked a new offensive of Islam against Christianity. Not only was the security of the pilgrimages to the Holy Land compromised, but the very existence of the Holy Sepulchre and of the Latin establishments in Jerusalem again became questionable. Finally, the destruction of the churches of Asia Minor was an occasion of fear and humiliation for all Christians. It thus seems that from the time of the first disasters the idea of an expedition to aid Constantinople and Jerusalem was coming to life in the West.

This idea was, furthermore, stirred up by the Byzantine Emperors themselves. In

From Louis Bréhier, *L'Église et L'Orient au moyen âge: Les Croisades*, Second Edition (Paris, 1907), pp. 50–54. Reprinted with permission of the Librairie Victor Lecoffre. [Editor's Translation]

1073 Michael VII wrote in this vein to Pope Gregory VII and promised the pope a reunion of the Greek church with the Holy See. The pope at first gave this invitation a favorable reception. In a letter dated February 2, 1074, he called upon Count William of Bourgogne to go to defend Constantinople, which was being threatened by the Infidels. On March 1, in an encyclical addressed to all the faithful, he announced to them the danger run by "the Christian empire" and called upon them to let him know through ambassadors the decisions which they made. The pope immediately received proposals for aid, for in his letter to Count William VI of Poitiers he thanks the count for his offer, although the news of a victory over the Turks caused the expedition to be postponed. On the other hand, a letter addressed to Henry [IV], King of the Romans, breathes a new enthusiasm for the holy war. Gregory announces that the Italians and the ultramontanes have responded to his requests and that he is ready to march in person at the head of an army of 50,000 men to rescue the East and the Holy Sepulchre and at the same time to bring the dissident churches back to Christian unity. Before his departure he confides to Henry IV the defence of the Roman church.

Thus Pope Gregory VII, whose political and religious views are so remarkable for their keen vision, clearly saw the West's interest in opposing the progress of Islam and the eventual ruin of the Byzantine Empire. Undoubtedly the expedition which he planned did not have all of the characteristics of a Crusade. In his letters the question is less that of the conquest of the Holy Sepulchre than of the defence of Constantinople and the reunion of the dissident churches. No special indulgence is promised to the faithful who take up arms. But in spite of these differences, the letters of Gregory VII nevertheless lay out the first plan for a holy war which had been conceived in the West. In the midst of the diversity and divisions which characterized the feudal world of the eleventh century,

the pope alone remained conscious of Christian unity and of the common interests of all the faithful. In the face of dangers posed by the Muslim aggression, not only in the East, but also in Sicily and in Spain, the pope wished to assemble a force able to save Christendom and he saw in the reunion of the dissident Churches the necessary condition for a general alliance of all Christian powers. Circumstances prevented the pope from realising this great idea. Gregory VII was soon involved in the investiture struggle (1076) and in an alliance with the Normans of Italy, who were enemies of the Byzantine Empire. [The Emperors] Nicephorus Boteniates (1078–1081) and Alexius Comnenus [1081–1118] showed themselves hostile to the reunion of the two churches. The idea of Western intervention, however, was not lost and a fact which has long passed unnoticed seems to bear witness that it always entered into the plans of the government at Constantinople. In 1083 Euthymius, Patriarch of Jerusalem, who was at that time in the Byzantine Empire, was commissioned by Alexius Comnenus to go to Thessalonica to negotiate peace with Bohemond, Prince of Taranto, who had invaded imperial territory. The choice of this messenger is significant: one may suppose that among the arguments which were destined to secure the acquiescence of the Normans, those concerning the situation of Jerusalem and the common defence of Christendom must have carried a certain weight. It can thus be affirmed that in 1088, at the time of the accession of Urban II, the idea of the holy war of all Christians against the Muslims was, so to speak, floating in the air. The immediate Turkish danger impelled Gregory VII to formulate the idea first, but it is really the spontaneous expression of the enthusiasm for the Holy Land which centuries of uninterrupted pilgrimages and the memories of the greatness of Charlemagne had impressed on the heart of Western Christians. If one misunderstands the value of this past, it is impossible to explain the origin of the Crusades.

Popular Response to the Crusade

PAUL ROUSSET

Paul Rousset, a Swiss scholar, has worked principally on the popular psychology of the Crusade as revealed in medieval literature. His book, *The Origins and Characteristics of the First Crusade*, attempts to define and evaluate the appeal of the Crusade to its participants. Rousset has, in addition, written a short general history of the Crusades (*L'histoire des croisades:* Paris, 1957) and delivered a paper on the idea of the Crusade to the Tenth International Congress of Historical Sciences at Rome in 1955.

THE question of the origins of the first Crusade remains in dispute. What are its remote sources? What are its immediate causes? What was the role of Urban II? . . . We have recalled the growing importance of the papacy in the eleventh century and have indicated the designs which apparently stirred Urban II to preach the Crusade: the wish to take the offensive against Islam by a strategic diversion, the desire to reunite the two churches, the idea of an internal diversion, that is to say, the substitution of an external, holy war for internal, criminal wars [among Christians]. There are still other causes: help for the Christians of the East, adventurousness, the appeal of the rich and mysterious East, the established pattern of warfare against the Saracens (the pre-crusades), the necessity of liberating the Holy Land and the Holy Sepulchre.

All of these "classical" causes remain true, but we believe that it is necessary to throw some of them into relief, namely the [themes of] the Holy Land and the internal diversion. The Holy Land is what makes Urban II's expedition a Crusade, thus giving a new character to the holy war. The chroniclers were quite aware of this. Their narratives are full of impassioned descriptions of Palestine, which they depict not only as a geographical and stra-

tegic goal, but also as the exalted spot to which the Spirit has called them. The Holy Land and, in particular, the Holy Sepulchre makes a real appeal to the hearts of the knights. For the men of the twelfth century it was a fatherland whose exiled children they were.

The argument in support of the internal diversion needs to be underscored, for its importance was decisive. All of the chroniclers depict the Crusade as a means of salvation for knights who are accustomed to throw themselves into feudal wars; these criminal wars will be replaced by a holy war. The Crusade, since it does not suffer from the grave [spiritual] defects of other wars, is a kind of anti-war; it is on another plane from [ordinary] war. Wars are deadly for all who take part in them, victors and vanquished alike; while the Crusade saves both those who participate in it and also Christendom itself, which feudal warriors have abandoned. The Crusade is not only an anti-war, it is peace: the peace of God, which is finally attained.

The peace movements, that is, movements to establish an organization able to limit, if not to halt, feudal wars, began in the tenth century and developed further in the eleventh century. Councils decreed sanctions and proposed measures which were accepted in one place, ignored in an-

From Paul Rousset, *Les Origines et les Caractères de la première Croisade* (Neuchâtel, 1945), pp. 194–198. Reprinted with the permission of Editions de la Baconnière. [Editor's Translation]

other. Under the date August 25, 1054, the Council of Narbonne decreed: "A Christian who kills another Christian spills the blood of Christ." Urban II was first among the popes to interest himself deeply in the Truce of God and at the Council of Clermont he renewed and generalized the decrees of the Council of Narbonne. It is after dealing with the matter of the Peace and Truce of God that Urban proclaimed the Crusade. Thus the Crusade appears to follow the Truce of God and, indeed, to develop from it. Is this true? What connections are there between these two institutions, both of them universalized by the pope's will? If one considers only the chronology and certain aspects of the matter, one might be tempted to agree with Luchaire: "The great work of the Crusade would only be possible if the country ceased to be upset by wars." But, so to speak, this is to take the cause for the result. All of the documentation of the Crusade militates against this concept. The Crusade is not the outcome of the institutions of peace. Rather, the Crusade is better seen as another aspect of the Peace and one which proves to be its downfall. We think, then, that in the thought of its inventor and its preachers the Crusade was supposed to secure for the Western world a peace which conciliar decrees were unable to provide. The Crusade comes at the end of the evolution of the peace institutions. It is a supreme effort to establish a solid peace and a durable truce. At the same time, the Crusade is a sign that the peace institutions did not suffice, that it was necessary, not to suppress them, but to extend them by adding another institution, also international, but of quite a different character. The Crusade appears, then, as the unexpected result of the peace efforts of the eleventh century and as the grand result of those efforts. The Crusade is an anti-war, a new war with characteristics different from feudal wars. One may even say, with regard to its relationship to the Peace and Truce of God, that the Crusade is a peace. The sacred character of the Crusade is explained

in part by these relationships. Just think of the benefits which the Crusaders conferred on Christendom by leaving it! The way in which the chroniclers insist on contrasting this new war to the old wars, the apologies of the poets for the knight who is constantly at war with the Saracens, St. Bernard's defence of the knight-monk — all of these show the rather considerable significance of the Crusade: it ushers in a real political and social revolution. Henceforth feudal wars are regarded by those who recall them as scandalous wars, as wars which betrayed Christianity. For two centuries the Crusades — although they were frequently political and colonial enterprises as well — recalled to knights, who were tempted to forget, that internal wars were criminal. At the same time they gave the West peace for several years and thus were like a series of Truces of God.

The Crusade brought peace to Christendom and at the same time provided unity. . . . This was unity in two areas: unity in the army of Crusaders, composed of contingents from several nations, and unity in the West, which was delivered from its endemic wars. In Urban II's thought, apparently, the Crusade should also have restored unity to the Eastern and Western Churches. In this regard the Crusade was a total failure, for it confirmed the division which had already long separated the two Churches.

All of the causes of the Crusades which historians have discovered and which we have just reviewed are good ones, but they do not suffice to explain an event of such magnitude. Furthermore, these same causes in other periods would have produced holy wars, but not a Crusade. What do these wars lack to merit the name "Crusade"? What was lacking in all of the Crusades after the first one? The thing that was missing was what gave the First Crusade its special nature, its specificity, its characteristics. What was missing was a psychological element, a whole spirituality. However, the Crusade could only have all of these things which made up its "personality" at a favorable time. This truth, simple as it may be, must be examined more closely.

A movement as wide-spread and as new as the Crusade requires a certain singleness of spirit and of heart — almost a response before the event. In thinking about it as a war, we are first of all aware of all the slow preparations, of the habits and tastes and the experiences gained here and there (the pre-crusades). But we are additionally aware of a spiritual disposition, of a whole psychological climate. The well-known saying: "The Crusade was impossible without the *Song of Roland*" contains a profound truth. The Crusade could only have been undertaken and the *Song of Roland* could only have been composed at a period when the Crusading ideal could be realized among men and could stir people up. A slow ripening of the spirit had made Charlemagne a universal hero, the leader of Christendom. Charlemagne is regarded as Christendom's authentic leader, as a champion who is delegated to carry on Christendom's external warfare, acting in its name. The road to Jerusalem is Charlemagne's road and, if one believes Robert the Monk, Urban II himself, acting at Clermont as Christendom's leader, made reference to Charlemagne. The Crusaders are soldiers of Charlemagne, his posthumous army: they are the elect, the people chosen for this task. Epic poetry brought this feeling home to the knights of the West and made them ready to accept Urban II's appeal. This period, the end of the eleventh century, is important in the history of thought: it is the period of the Crusade, the period, we may say, at which the Crusade is possible, not as a political undertaking, not because of the political situation, but as a true Crusade, in virtue of a particular cast of mind and of heart.

One cannot emphasize sufficiently this aspect of the problem. The Crusade is a product of its time and of quite a limited time — a time which is above all defined by its mentality and its ideals. The political, economic, and military motives should

not be overlooked, but they are not sufficient to explain a war in which psychological elements and religious ideals play such a large part . . . . The Crusaders did not respond solely to political motives — not even to motives of high politics — nor did they respond solely to motives of personal interest. They also responded (and some of them responded above all else) to spiritual motives: they were moved by a certain cast of mind, by certain passions, and by certain tastes. This cast of mind, these spiritual motives are what prevailed in the Crusade. It was these considerations which could lift people out of their customary ways and carry them away from their homes. It was these considerations which could bolster them up through a difficult venture. The First Crusade is unthinkable outside of the period in which it was born. It is a product of that period. The study of the chronicles, charters, annals, letters, and *chansons de geste* shows us a war which is underwritten primarily by a mentality, a psychology; a war which takes its force from religious thought. At the origin of the Crusade, then, there is an ability to accept the spirit of the Crusade, a disposition to live this adventure. The origins of the Crusade are within medieval society. The origins spring basically from the thoughts, tastes, passions, and ideals which are peculiar to Christians of this period.

This spontaneous reaction, these favorable predispositions, however, are not enough. History is not made without the human will, without the cooperation of the intelligence, without free participation. Monsieur Bréhier remarks that "If the whole history of Europe in the tenth and eleventh centuries explains how the Crusading spirit was born and developed, . . . then the Crusade itself is an historical accident which could in no way have been foreseen with certainty and which is due alone to the initiative of Pope Urban II." The Crusade is at one and the same time the result of a long historical development, the product of an evolution, and an "historical accident," the creation of a man and the product of a free will. Urban II was the man and his was the will. He invented an entirely new enterprise, which upset customary habits and transformed society, but which also responded to the internal dispositions of that society.

The genius of Urban II lay in recognizing in the society of his time the capacity to accept the call to the Crusade and to see how the Crusade could bring peace to the West. At Clermont the pope spoke to a people who were ready to take up the idea of the Crusade, to a people who were Crusaders without being aware of it. He disclosed to them the ideal lurking in their hearts. The influence of Urban II was decisive in the year 1095. At the time everything seemed opposed to a great undertaking which presupposed the unity of Christendom. Everything seemed hostile to a new responsibility for Urban II at a time when an anti-pope continued to fight against him. But what could have been more majestic than Urban's long journey through France, from town to town, from monastery to monastery. At the moment he chose, on November 27 in the Champ-Herm at Clermont, Urban II preached to the crowd of clerics and laymen and proclaimed the Crusade. The famous cry, "God

wills it" was to be taken up by the knights themselves as they discovered the Crusading spirit which was already in them, which the pope's voice had revealed to them. Here everything we have said about the preparatory cast of mind and the interior dispositions on the one hand and about man's free will and initiative on the other hand came together at once.

The Crusade is thus the result of a twofold call, as Christendom becomes aware of a common task which is to be accomplished. This awareness involves the common consensus of Christendom: this fact seems to us worthy of being noted once again. It is not a question of the thought of a few theoreticians. Rather, it is a matter of the consensus of thought of a great multitude of people — a militant and thoughtful group of clerics, knights, merchants, poets — so far as the consensus is definable. The literature of the Crusade, since it deals with this consensus and since it describes this ideology better than other texts, should be given considered attention. The chroniclers who describe the Crusade and the poets who sing about the holy war can bear a significant witness to an important movement in medieval thought. This is the witness which we have tried to evaluate.

The Appeal of the Crusade to the Poor

NORMAN COHN

Norman Cohn was born in London in 1915 and was educated at Christ Church College, Oxford. His research interests have lain principally in the field of medieval French literature. He has taught at the University of Glasgow and at Magill University College, Londonderry; since 1960 he has been Professor of French at King's College in Newcastle-Upon-Tyne. In addition to his study of *The Pursuit of the Millennium*, Professor Cohn has written two other books: *Gold Khan and Other Siberian Legends* (1946) and *Jean de Meun and the Roman de la Rose* (1961).

. . . Urban II, when he summoned the chivalry of Christendom to the Crusade, . . . released in the masses hopes and hatreds which were to express themselves in ways quite alien to the aims of papal policy.

Gregory [VII] . . . had planned to lead an army of Christian knights to the relief of Byzantium, much harassed by the invasions of the Seldjuk Turks. When in 1095, ten years after Gregory's death, Urban made his famous appeal at Clermont, his primary object was still to provide the Byzantines with the reinforcements they needed in order to drive the infidel from Asia Minor; for he hoped that in return the Eastern Church would acknowledge the supremacy of Rome, so that the unity of Christendom would be restored. In the second place he was concerned to indicate to the nobility, particularly of his native France, an alternative outlet for martial energies which were still constantly bringing devastation upon the land. The moment was appropriate, for the Council of Clermont had been largely concerned with the Truce of God, that ingenious device by which the Church had for half a century been trying to limit feudal warfare. In addition to clerics a large number of lesser nobles had accordingly come to Clermont; and it was primarily to these that, on the last day of the Council, the Pope addressed himself. To those who would take part in the Crusade Urban offered impressive rewards. A knight who with pious intent took the Cross would earn a remission from temporal penalties for all his sins; if he died in battle he would earn remission of his sins. And there were to be material as well as spiritual rewards. Over-population was not confined to the peasantry; one of the reasons for the perpetual wars between nobles was a real shortage of land. Younger sons had often no patrimony at all and had no choice but to seek their fortune. According to one account Urban himself contrasted the actual indigence of many nobles with the prosperity which they would enjoy when they had conquered fine new fiefs in southern lands. Whether he did so or not, this was certainly a consideration which weighed with many crusaders. And nevertheless it is clear that already amongst the prelates and priests and nobles who heard Urban's appeal at Clermont something was at work which was not simply an expectation of individual gain, whether material or spiritual. As the assembly listened it was swept by emotions of overwhelming power. Thousands cried with one voice: *"Deus le volt!"* — "It is God's will!" Crowding around the Pope and kneeling before him they begged leave to take part

From *The Pursuit of the Millennium* by Norman Cohn. Oxford University Press, Inc., 1957, pp. 40–52. Reprinted by permission of Oxford University Press and Martin Secker and Warburg, Limited.

in the holy war. A cardinal fell on his knees and recited the *Confiteor* in the name of the whole multitude and as they echoed it after him many burst into tears and many were seized with convulsive trembling. For a brief moment there reigned in that predominantly aristocratic assembly an atmosphere of collective enthusiasm such as was to become normal in the contingents of common folk which were formed later.

For the appeal at Clermont was only the beginning of an agitation which was at once taken up by many preachers. The Crusade continued to be preached to the nobility by Urban himself, who spent several months travelling through France for the purpose, and by the bishops who had returned from Clermont to their dioceses. It was also preached to the common people by a number of *prophetae,* men who though not equipped with any official authorisation had the prestige which always surrounded the miracle-working ascetic. The most celebrated of these was Peter the Hermit. Born near Amiens, he had passed a sternly ascetic life, first as a monk and then as a hermit. He went barefoot and never touched meat or wine. A small thin man with a long grey beard, he possessed a commanding presence and great eloquence; so that, according to one who knew him, his every word and act seemed half-divine. Over the masses he exercised an irresistible fascination. People flocked around him, struggling to pluck from the ass he rode on a single hair to treasure as a relic. Myths proliferated around his life-story. Before ever the Pope had spoken, it was said, Peter had been to Jerusalem. In the Church of the Holy Sepulchre Christ had appeared to him and had given him a letter commissioning him to summon the Crusade. Peter seems to have contributed to the myth by carrying the Heavenly Letter with him wherever he preached. His success as a propagandist was immense. As he passed through northern France an army of crusaders sprang into being. People hastened to sell their belongings to buy weapons and travelling-kit; then, having no longer any means of subsistence, they began to move off. In March, 1096 — four months before the official Crusade of the barons was ready — Peter crossed from French into German territory at the head of the horde which he had inspired. And meanwhile other hordes were forming around other leaders in northern France, in Flanders and along the Rhine.

The army which the Pope had envisaged was to have consisted of knights with their retainers, all of them trained in warfare and properly equipped; and most of the nobles who responded to the papal summons did in fact prepare themselves in a sober and realistic manner for the campaign. The hordes conjured up by the preachings of the *prophetae,* on the other hand, consisted of people whose lack of military qualifications was only equalled by their impetuosity. They had indeed no reason to delay and every reason to hurry. Almost all of them were poor; and they came from those overcrowded regions where the lot of the poor was perpetual insecurity. Moreover during the decade 1085–1095 life had been much harder even than usual. Precisely in northeastern France and western Germany there had been an almost unbroken series of floods, droughts and famines. Since 1089 the population had also been living in constant terror of a particularly unpleasant form of plague which would suddenly and without apparent cause strike at town or village, bringing an agonising death to the majority of the inhabitants. The mass reactions to these calamities had been the usual ones: people had clustered in devotional and penitential groups around hermits and other holy men and had embarked on a collective quest for salvation. The sudden appearance of the *prophetae* preaching the Crusade gave these afflicted masses the chance to form salvationist groups on a much vaster scale and at the same time to escape from lands where life had become intolerable. Men and women alike hastened to join the new movement. Often whole families would move together, with the children and household chattels loaded on to carts. And as the hordes grew they were further swollen by all kinds of nondescript adventurers — by renegade monks, women disguised as men and many robbers and brigands.

To these hordes the Crusade meant something quite different from what it meant to the Pope. The *pauperes,* as the chroniclers called them, were not greatly interested in assisting the Christians of Byzantium, but they were passionately interested in reaching, capturing and occupying Jerusalem. The city which was the holiest city in the world for Christians had been in the hands of Moslems for some four and a half centuries. Although the possibility of recapturing it seems to have played little part in Urban's original plan, it was this prospect that intoxicated the masses of the poor. In their eyes the Crusade was an armed and militant pilgrimage, the greatest and most sublime of pilgrimages. For centuries a pilgrimage to the Holy Sepulchre had been regarded as a singularly efficacious form of penance and during the eleventh century such pilgrimages had been undertaken collectively: penitents tended to travel no longer singly or in small groups but in bands organised hierarchically under a leader. Sometimes — notably in 1033 and 1064 — mass pilgrimages had taken place, involving many thousands of people. In 1033 at least, the first to go had been the poor and amongst them there had been some who went with the intention of staying in Jerusalem until their death. In the Crusade too the poor, or many of them, had no thought of ever returning to their homes: they meant to take Jerusalem from the infidel and by settling in it turn it into a Christian city. Everyone who took part in the Crusade wore a cross sewn on to his outer garment — the first badge worn by an army in post-Classical times and the first step towards modern military uniforms; but whereas for the knights this cross was a symbol of Christian victory in a military expedition

of limited duration, the poor thought rather of the sentence: "Take up the Cross and follow me!" For them the Crusade was above all a collective *imitatio Christi,* a mass sacrifice which was to be rewarded by a mass apotheosis at Jerusalem.

For the Jerusalem which obsessed their imagination was no mere earthly city but rather the symbol of a prodigious hope. It had been so ever since the messianic ideal of the Hebrews had first begun to take shape in the eighth century B.C. Already through the mouth of Isaiah the Lord had bidden the Hebrews: "Rejoice ye with Jerusalem, and be glad with her . . . That ye may suck, and be satisfied with the breasts of her consolations; that ye may milk out, and be delighted with the abundance of her glory. . . . Behold, I will extend peace to her like a river . . . then shall ye suck, ye shall be borne upon her sides, and be dandled upon her knees. As one whom his mother comforteth, so will I comfort you: and ye shall be comforted in Jerusalem." In the prophecies of the post-exilic period and in the apocalypses the messianic kingdom is imagined as centered on a future Jerusalem which has been rebuilt in great magnificence. These ancient Jewish phantasies all went to reinforce the great emotional significance which Jerusalem would in any case have possessed for medieval Christians. When, a generation after the event, a monk composed the appeal which he imagined Urban to have made at Clermont, he made the Pope speak of the Holy City not simply as the palace made forever illustrious by the Advent, Passion and Ascension of Christ but also as "the navel of the world, the land fruitful above all others, like another paradise of delights," "the royal city placed in the centre of the world," now held captive, demanding help, yearning for liberation. Moreover even for theologians Jerusalem was also a "figure" or symbol of the heavenly city "like unto a stone most precious" which according to the Book of Revelation was to replace it at the end of time. No wonder that — as contemporaries noted — in the minds of simple folk the idea of the earthly Jerusalem became so confused with and transfused by that of the Heavenly Jerusalem that the Palestinian city seemed itself a miraculous realm, abounding both in spiritual and in material blessings. And no wonder that when the masses of the poor set off on their long pilgrimage the children cried out at every town and castle: "Is that Jerusalem?" — while high in the heavens there was seen a mysterious city with vast multitudes hurrying towards it.

While in northern France, Flanders and the Rhine valley the poor formed themselves into autonomous bands, in that other densely populated, highly urbanised area, Provence, they streamed into the army of the Count, Raymond of Toulouse. As a result there developed in that army an exaltation as intense as that which prevailed in the hordes which followed the *prophetae*. Alike in north and south, the poor who went on the Crusade regarded themselves as the *elite* of the crusaders, a people chosen by God as the barons had not been chosen. When at a critical moment in the siege of Antioch St Andrew brought the glad tidings that the Holy Lance was buried in one of the churches in the town, it was to a poor Provençal peasant that he appeared. And when the peasant, conscious of his lowly status, hesitated to transmit the news to the noble leaders, the saint reassured him: "God has chosen you (poor folk) from amongst all peoples, as ears of wheat are gathered from amidst a field of oats. For in merit and in grace you surpass all who shall come after you, as much as gold surpasses silver." Raymond of Aguilers, who tells the story, comes nearest of the chroniclers to sharing the outlook of the poor. It seemed to him natural that when some of the poor are killed, miraculous crosses should be found on their shoulderblades; and when he speaks of the *plebs pauperum* it is always with a certain awe, as the Chosen of the Lord.

The self-exaltation of the poor emerges still more clearly from the curious stories, compounded of fact and legend, which were told of the people called "Tafurs." A large part — probably by far the larger part — of the People's Crusade perished on its journey across Europe; but enough survived to form in Syria and Palestine a corps of vagabonds — which is what the mysterious word "Tafur" seems to have meant. Barefoot, shaggy, clad in ragged sackcloth, covered with sores and filth, living on roots and grass and also at times on the roasted corpses of their enemies, the Tafurs were such a ferocious band that any country they passed through was utterly devastated. Too poor to afford swords and lances, they wielded clubs weighted with lead, pointed sticks, knives, hatchets, shovels, hoes and catapults. When they charged into battle they gnashed their teeth as though they meant to eat their enemies alive as well as dead. The Moslems, though they faced the crusading barons fearlessly, were terrified of the Tafurs, whom they called "no Franks, but living devils." The Christian chroniclers themselves — clerics or knights whose main interest was in the doings of the princes — while admitting the effectiveness of the Tafurs in battle clearly regarded them with misgiving and embarrassment. Yet if one turns to a vernacular epic written from the standpoint of the poor, one finds the Tafurs portrayed as a Holy People and "worth far more than the knights."

The Tafurs are shown as having a king, *le roi Tafur*. He is said to have been a Norman knight who had discarded horse, arms and armour in favour of sackcloth and a scythe. At least in the beginning he was an ascetic for whom poverty had all the mystical value which it was to possess for St Francis and his disciples. Periodically King Tafur would inspect his men. Any who were found to have money about them were expelled from the company and sent off to buy arms and join the professional army under the barons; while those who had with greatest conviction renounced all property were admitted to membership of the "college" or inner circle of followers. It was precisely because of their poverty that the Tafurs believed themselves destined to take the Holy City: "The poorest shall take it: this is a sign to show clearly that the Lord God does not care for presumptuous and faithless men." Yet though the poor made a merit of their poverty, they were full of cupidity. Booty captured from the infidel was not felt to diminish their claims on divine favour but rather to prove how real that favour was. After a successful skirmish outside Antioch the Provençal poor "gallop on horseback amongst the tents to show their companions how their poverty is at an end; others, dressed in two or three silken garments, praise God as the bestower of victory and of gifts." As King Tafur leads the final assault on Jerusalem he cries: "Where are the poor folk who want property? Let them come with me! . . . For today with God's help I shall win enough to load many a mule!" And later, when the Moslems carry their treasures round the walls of the captured city in an effort to lure the Christians out into the open, we are shown the Tafurs unable to hold back. "Are we in prison?" cries the King; "They bring treasure and we dare not take it! . . . What do I care if I die, since I am doing what I want to do?" And calling on "St Lazarus" — the Lazarus of the parable, of whom the poor in the Middle Ages made their patron saint — he leads his horde out of the city to catastrophe.

In each captured city the Tafurs looted everything they could lay hands on, raped the Moslem women and carried out indiscriminate massacres. The official leaders of the Crusade had no authority over them at all. When the Emir of Antioch protested about the cannibalism of the Tafurs, the princes could only admit apologetically: "All of us together cannot tame King Tafur." The barons seem in fact to have been somewhat frightened of the Tafurs and to have taken care to be well armed whenever they came near them. That no

doubt was the truth of the matter; but in the stories which are told from the standpoint of the poor the great princes regard their Tafur king not so much with anxiety as with humility, even with reverence. We find King Tafur urging on the hesitant barons to attack Jerusalem: "My lords, what are we doing? We are delaying overlong our assault on this city and this evil race. We are behaving like false pilgrims. If it rested with me and with the poor alone, the pagans would find us the worst neighbours they ever had!" The princes are so impressed that they ask him to lead the first attack; and when, covered with wounds, he is carried from the battlefield, they gather anxiously around him. But King Tafur is shown as something more than simply the mightiest of warriors. Often he appears in close association with a *propheta* — in one version it is Peter the Hermit, in another a fictitious bishop who bears that emblem which the poor had made their own, the Holy Lance. And he himself clearly possesses a supernatural quality which sets him above all princes. When — in the story as edited for the poor — Godfrey of Bouillon is to become King of Jerusalem, the barons choose King Tafur as 'the highest one' to perform the coronation. He performs it by giving Godfrey a branch of thorns in memory of the Crown of Thorns: and Godfrey does homage and swears to hold Jerusalem as a fief from King Tafur and God alone. And when the barons, feeling that they have endured enough, hasten back to their wives and their domains, King Tafur will not see Jerusalem abandoned but pledges himself to stay, with his army of poor, to defend the new king and his kingdom. In these purely imaginary incidents the beggarking becomes the symbol of the immense, unreasoning hope which had carried the *plebs pauperum* through unspeakable hardships to the Holy City.

The realisation of that hope demanded human sacrifice on a vast scale — not only the self-immolation of the crusaders but also the massacre of the infidel. Although

Pope and princes might intend a campaign with limited objectives, in reality the campaign tended constantly to become what the common people wanted it to be: a war to exterminate "the sons of whores," 'the race of Cain,' as King Tafur called the Moslems. It was not unknown for crusaders to seize all the peasants of a certain area and offer them the choice of being either immediately converted to Christianity or immediately killed — "having achieved which, our Franks returned full of joy." The fall of Jerusalem was followed by a holocaust; except for the governor and his bodyguard, who managed to buy their lives and were escorted from the city, every Moslem — man, woman and child — was killed. In and around the Temple of Solomon "the horses waded in blood up to their knees, nay up to the bridle. It was a just and wonderful judgment of God that the same place should receive the blood of those whose blasphemies it had so long carried up to God." As for the Jews of Jerusalem, when they took refuge in their chief synagogue the building was set on fire and they were all burnt alive. Weeping with joy and singing songs of praise the crusaders marched in procession to the Church of the Holy Sepulchre. "O new day, new day and exultation, new and everlasting gladness. . . . That day, famed through all centuries to come, turned all our suffering and hardships into joy and exultation; that day, the confirmation of Christianity, the annihilation of paganism, the renewal of our faith!" But a handful of the infidel still survived: they had taken refuge on the roof of the mosque of al-Aqsa. The celebrated crusader Tancred had promised them their lives in exchange for a heavy ransom and had given them his banner as a safe-conduct. But Tancred could only watch with helpless fury while common soldiers scaled the walls of the mosque and beheaded every man and woman save those who threw themselves off the roof to their death.

If one bears these happenings in mind it seems natural enough that the first great massacre of European Jews should also have occurred during the First Crusade. The official crusading army, consisting of the barons and their retainers, had no part in this massacre, which was carried out entirely by the hordes which formed in the wake of the *prophetae*. As the Crusade came into being, observes one chronicler, "peace was established very firmly on all sides and the Jews were at once attacked in the towns where they lived." It is said that already at the very beginning of the crusading agitation Jewish communities in Rouen and other French towns were given the choice between conversion and massacre. But it was in the episcopal cities along the Rhine that the most violent attacks took place. Here, as along all the trade routes of western Europe, Jewish merchants had been settled for centuries; and because of their economic usefulness they had always enjoyed the special favour of the archbishops. But by the close of the eleventh century in all these cities tension between the townsmen and their ecclesiastical lords was already giving rise to a general social turbulence. It was an atmosphere which proved as favourable to the *prophetae* of the Crusade as it was shortly to prove to [another popular preacher,] Tanchelm.

At the beginning of May, 1096, crusaders camping outside Speyer planned to attack the Jews in their synagogue on the Sabbath. In this they were foiled and they were only able to kill a dozen Jews in the streets. The Bishop lodged the rest in his castle and had some of the murderers punished. At Worms the Jews were less fortunate. Here too they turned for help to the Bishop and the well-to-do burghers, but these were unable to protect them when men from the People's Crusade arrived and led the townsfolk in an attack on the Jewish quarter. The synagogue was sacked, houses were looted and all their adult occupants who refused baptism were killed. As for 'the children, some were killed, others taken away to be baptised and brought up as Christians. Some Jews had taken shelter in the Bishop's castle and when that too was attacked the Bishop offered to baptise them and so save their lives; but the entire community preferred to commit suicide. In all, some eight hundred Jews are said to have perished at Worms.

At Mainz, where there lived the largest Jewish community in Germany, events took much the same course. There too the Jews were at first protected by the Archbishop, the chief lay lord and the richer burghers, but in the end were forced by the crusaders, supported by the poorer townsfolk, to choose between baptism and death. The Archbishop and his staff fled, in fear of their lives. More than a thousand Jews and Jewesses perished, either by suicide or at the hands of the crusaders. From the Rhine cities a band of crusaders moved to Trier. The Archbishop delivered a sermon demanding that the Jews be spared; but as a result he himself had to flee from the church. Here too, although some Jews accepted baptism, the great majority perished. The crusaders moved on to Metz, where they killed some more Jews, and then returned in mid-June to Cologne. The Jewish community had gone into hiding in neighbouring villages; but they were discovered by the crusaders and massacred in hundreds. Meanwhile other bands of crusaders, making their way eastwards, had imposed baptism by force on the communities of Regensburg and Prague. In all, the number of Jews who perished in the months of May and June, 1096, is estimated at between four and eight thousand.

It was the beginning of a tradition. While in 1146 the Second Crusade was being prepared by King Louis VII and the French nobility, the populace in Normandy and Picardy killed Jews. Meanwhile a renegade monk called Rudolph made his way from Hainaut to the Rhine, where he summoned the masses to join in a People's Crusade and to make a start by killing the Jews. As at the time of the First Crusade, the common people were being driven to desperation by famine. Like every successful *propheta*, Rudolph was believed to perform miracles and to be favoured with divine revelations; and hungry multitudes flocked to him just as, in remote Brittany, multitudes were at that very time attaching themselves to the heresiarch Eudes de l'Etoile. It was still the episcopal cities with their bitter internal conflicts — Cologne, Mainz, Worms, Speyer and also this time Strasbourg and, when the Crusade passed through it, Würzburg — that proved the most fertile ground for anti-Jewish agitation. From them the movement spread to many other towns in Germany and France. The Jews turned for protection, as they had done half a century earlier, to the bishops and prosperous burghers. These did what they could to help; but the *pauperes* were not to be so easily deterred. In many towns the populace was on the point of open insurrection and it seemed that another overwhelming catastrophe was about to descend on the Jews. At that point St Bernard intervened and, with the full weight of his prestige, insisted that the massacre must stop.

Even St Bernard with all his extraordinary reputation as a holy man and a worker of miracles, was scarcely able to check the popular fury. When he confronted Rudolph at Mainz and, as an abbot, ordered him back to his monastery, the common people almost took up arms to protect their *propheta*. Thereafter, the massacre of Jews was to remain a normal feature of popular, as distinct from knightly, crusades; and it is clear enough why. Although the *pauperes* looted freely from the Jews they killed (as they did from the Moslems), booty was certainly not their main object. It is a Hebrew chronicle that records how during the Second Crusade the crusaders appealed to the Jews: 'Come to us, so that we become one single people'; and there seems no doubt that a Jew could always save both life and property by accepting baptism. On the other hand it was said that whoever killed a Jew who refused baptism had all his sins forgiven him; and there were those who felt unworthy to start on a crusade at all until they had killed at least one such. Some of the crusaders' own comments have been preserved: "We have set out to march a long way to fight the enemies of God in the East, and behold, before our very eyes are his worst foes, the Jews. They must be dealt with first." And again: "You are the descendants of those who killed and hanged our God." Moreover (God) himself said: "The day will yet dawn when my children will come and avenge my blood. We are his children and it is our task to carry out his vengeance upon you, for you showed yourselves obstinate and blasphemous towards him. . . . (God) has abandoned you and has turned his radiance upon us and has made us his own."

Here, unmistakably, speaks the same conviction which tried to turn the First Crusade into an annihilation of Islam.

The Clergy, the Poor and the Non-Combatants
on the First Crusade

WALTER PORGES

Walter Porges is an American scholar, born in 1918. He received both
his undergraduate and graduate training at the University of Chicago and he
has since taught at that University, as well as at Connecticut College, Lawrence
College, and the Los Angeles City College. He was a Fulbright Research
Fellow in Belgium in 1952–53.

WHEN Pope Urban preached the
First Crusade at Clermont, he did
not have in mind a purely military expedition. Ever since the time of Constantine,
large numbers of pious or adventurous pilgrims of both sexes had made their way to
the Holy Land. Although interrupted now
and again by the convulsions periodically
shaking the Levant, in the tenth and eleventh centuries the pilgrimages continued
to flourish. The pilgrims travelled mostly
in small groups, and apparently did not
bear arms, even for self-defense; but during the first half of the eleventh century,
the small pilgrim bands were supplemented
by larger enterprises, numbering several
hundred to several thousand participants.
The great German pilgrimage of 1064–
1065 included from seven to twelve thousand persons — the equivalent of a respect-
able medieval army.

The pope could not escape the influence
of this vigorous tradition. The petty feudal
wars of western Europe could not offer
him a model for his stupendous undertaking. The pilgrimage was the only large-
scale, long-distance expedition with which
he was familiar; moreover, he knew the
power of the pilgrim ideal. Therefore Urban combined the idea of the Palestine
pilgrimage with that of the holy war. He

implemented his plans for the recovery of
the Holy Land not by an appeal limited
to the chivalry of Europe, but by stirring
up the latent pilgrim enthusiasm which
pervaded all classes, raising it to an unprecedented pitch, and directing it into
new, more warlike channels. By arming
the pilgrimage the pope created the crusade.

The term *peregrinus*, the verb *pere-
grinari* now served to designate the crusader, as well as the pilgrim, and describe
his activity. The crusaders in the main
followed the land route through Hungary
and Bulgaria, and down the Balkans to
the Golden Horn, preferred by pilgrims
since the conversion of the Magyars. Of
those who took the alternate path through
Italy, many identified themselves even
more closely with pilgrim tradition. Some,
when they had worshipped at St. Peter's,
considered their vows fulfilled; others, deserted by their leaders in Calabria, 'took
up their pilgrim staves again, and igno-
miniously returned home.' The faithful,
who persisted to the end, had as their
reward the plenary indulgence, the usual
goal of pious pilgrims.

Urban's dependence upon the pilgrim
movement had its disadvantages. The crusade had before it a desperately difficult

From Walter Porges, "The Clergy, the Poor and the Non-Combatants on the First Crusade," *Spec-
ulum,* XXI (January, 1946), pp. 1–21. Reprinted by permission of The Medieval Academy of Amer-
ica. Footnotes have been omitted.

military task, and efficiency demanded a careful selection of recruits. But the new movement was caught betwixt and between: rooted in the pilgrimage, the crusade attracted large numbers of non-combatants, such as had always gone on pilgrimages; while as a military expedition the crusade found it inexpedient or even dangerous to admit very many of them.

Urban was aware of the contradiction. Although he found the inclusion of noncombatants implicit in his crusade conception, and his appeal took their participation for granted, he took pains, nevertheless, to limit their number and supervise their selection. The pope laid down the rule that all persons were to consult their local clergy before going on crusade. In addition, he emphasized the need for fighting men, and for men wealthy enough to bear the cost of the journey, and discouraged the participation of the aged and sick. But he permitted women to go, if properly escorted, and reserved an especially important place for the clergy. Urban also invited the poor; not, however, as noncombatants, but as potential fighters, to be equipped and maintained by the charity of the wealthier crusaders. In this respect the pope's expectations were deceived. Before the campaign was half over, the poor had been reduced to a noncombatant or at best semi-combatant condition.

Unfortunately, the pilgrim tradition, reinforced by the deep enthusiasm roused by itinerant preachers, overwhelmed Urban's attempts to limit participation in the crusade. More than five premature expeditions, collectively termed the peasants' crusade, did not suffice to draw off the excess of unarmed and unfit. Some of these expeditions were reasonably well-armed and well-disciplined, and failed largely because they were premature. Others, however, were belated pilgrim excursions, best viewed as half-way stages between the unarmed pilgrimage and the crusade proper. Fired by a new and unrestrained zeal, they attracted a strange mixture of priests and laymen, women, children, and those wont to prey upon them, false prophets and simple-minded believers. Many of the participants were unarmed, and expected to overcome the Saracens by the direct intervention of God, rather than by the use of earthly weapons. Most of them left their bones on the plains of Hungary and Bulgaria, or were slaughtered by the Turks on the threshold of Asia Minor.

Nevertheless, there were more than enough noncombatants left over to swell the ranks of the main army. Urban's admonitions went unheeded. The aged and sick trudged along, seeking the earthly Jerusalem; campfollowers and harlots trailed as ever in the wake of the army. No information exists to justify even a rough estimate of the actual number of noncombatants. The chroniclers, who estimate the size of the army in very round numbers, scarcely honor any but the fighting men with more than passing mention, while all the descriptions of the army before it reached Nicaea seem vitiated by confusion with the peasants' crusade. But some information may be gleaned from Fulcher of Chartres' eyewitness account of the situation at Nicaea: 'Then out of many armies, one army was there created, which those who were skilled in reckoning estimated at six hundred thousand men fit for combat, of whom one hundred thousand were armed with cuirasses and helmets, not counting the unarmed, that is, clerics, monks, women and children.' There are pictorial numbers; but if only about one-sixth of the army was equipped with cuirasses and helmets, a large part of the remainder must have been half-armed poor. The form of the statement also suggests that the number of noncombatants was high.

If such was the condition of the army at Nicaea, it did not long remain unaltered. Thereafter the relative number of combatants fell steadily, and that of the noncombatants steadily increased. Battles and skirmishes took a constant toll of fighting men. Chronic illness reduced many to noncombatant status. Exhaustion of funds, necessitating the sale of arms and armor, might reduce a knight to a foot-soldier, or a foot-soldier to an unarmed pauper. That the greater part of the invalid and destitute soldiers never returned to full fighting efficiency is made plain by the fact that from the defeat of Kerbogha until the capture of Jerusalem (June, 1098 to July, 1099), the period of the greatest military supremacy ever enjoyed by the Christian army, the crusaders were sadly deficient in armed strength, and the unarmed host greatly outnumbered the fighters. Thus, in January, 1099, when the count of Toulouse wished to lead some of the poor on a plundering raid to obtain food, his intimates objected, saying, 'In the army [i.e., in Raymond's contingent] there are scarcely three hundred knights, and no great number of other armed men. . . .' Those opposing the diversion of the crusade to Egypt urged in protest: 'There are hardly fifteen hundred knights in the army, and no great number of armed foot-soldiers. . . .' Albert remarks that the crusaders marched on Jerusalem along the coast, instead of by way of Damascus, because the Turks were fewer along the seashore, and only twenty thousand men out of an army of fifty thousand were fit to fight. After the fall of Jerusalem, Raymond numbers the fighting men at not more than twelve thousand knights and nine thousand foot.

The noncombatants, too, suffered serious losses all along the way; but their numbers were swelled by a steady influx from the dwindling ranks of the fighters. In addition, the sturdy poor, in the beginning of some military value, early sank into such a miserable condition, that most of them were not called upon to fight except in great emergencies, and constituted a standing burden upon the army. Thus, by the time the siege of Antioch was well underway, the noncombatants — the sick, crippled, and destitute, the women, children, and clergy — had captured and maintained an absolute and overwhelming majority.

The form into which Urban cast the crusade, the inclusion of the clergy and other noncombatants, is evidence not only of his dependence upon pilgrim tradition, but of his belief that the Holy Land was not to be won by force of arms alone; that the power of the Word was greater than the power of the Sword; that the righteousness of the crusading army was a sure protection. As the spiritual heir of Gregory VII, how could the pope have thought otherwise? The main strength of the papacy was moral. Whatever the pope undertook, he could not depend upon earthly arms alone; and however disinterested his motives, he could not allow his project to become entirely secularized. Therefore Urban planned the crusade as an essentially Christian undertaking, in which the clergy were to play an important part from start to finish. The formal purpose of the crusade was religious — to free the Eastern Church. The crusaders were called by the clergy to take the cross; they consulted their parish priests before taking the irrevocable vow; they looked forward to a spiritual reward, the papal indulgence; and they were led, in so far as the crusade had a single leader, by the papal legate, Adhemar, bishop of Puy.

The clergy not only conceived and planned, but helped to organize the expedition. While Urban toured France, papal letters and legates travelled swiftly to England, Normandy, and Flanders, to Genoa and Bologna, exhorting, commanding, and persuading. When early in 1096 the squabbles of William Rufus with his brother Robert of Normandy threatened to prevent large-scale Norman participation, Urban sent his legate to negotiate a peace. As a result of his intervention, Robert mortgaged Normandy to William for ten thousand silver marks, and joined the crusade together with many of his vassals. Later in the same year the pope sent the bishops of Orange and Grenoble to preach the crusade at Genoa, and bring the formidable Genoese sea-power into the war. Their mission was successful, and a Genoese supply fleet gave the crusaders substantial aid at Antioch and Jerusalem.

Once upon the march, the crusaders maintained constant liaison with the western clergy, regarding them as their supporters and propagandists on the home front, and depending upon them for reinforcements in men and money. To such prelates as Manasses, archbishop of Rheims, they confided their needs and difficulties, entrusted their families and estates, addressed their pleas for masses and prayers. Many of them considered Urban the true head of the army. Whatever the political motives of the leaders, a vein of sincerity runs through their invitation to the pope to come and take charge of the expedition. With his seat at Antioch, he would direct operations against Jerusalem, extirpate heresy, and reduce the whole world to obedience. Urban refused, but aided the crusaders all he could by holding councils at Rome and Bari, and threatening those who failed to fulfill their vows with excommunication.

The pope, it seems, was not prepared to take up the bishop of Puy's unfinished task — a task which Adhemar had performed with exemplary patience and skill until his death at Antioch, August 1, 1098. Urban had invested the bishop with a sort of *maius imperium,* urging the crusaders to obey him completely in all matters pertaining to the crusade. But the papal legate was in no sense a generalissimo. Though not hesitating to plunge into battle whenever necessary, he did not pretend to exercise any authority over the actual conduct of the campaign. His real function was to preserve discipline and uphold enthusiasm among the rank and file, and compose the quarrels of the leaders, so as to gain their cooperation for the common good. Adhemar fully realized the delicacy of his position. The friend and neighbor of the count of Toulouse, with whom he travelled to Constantinople, he maintained, nevertheless, a neutral attitude in all disputes between the leaders, and used the language of exhortation, not of command. He was the special protector of the poor, and constantly urged the great folk to care

for them. The grief of the crusaders at Adhemar's death suffices to demonstrate the esteem in which he was held. Had he lived, the army might not have wasted so many months in useless sieges and petty bickerings after the fall of Antioch.

The papal legate was not the only representative of the church on crusade. Urban expected both regular and secular clergy to join in the movement — a fact made clear by his warning that the journey would have no spiritual value for those who went without the permission of their bishop or abbot. If the pope had not desired such permission to be granted in many instances, a flat prohibition would have been more appropriate than this mildly restrictive clause. His only concern was that clerical participants be properly qualified.

We have no more means of estimating the number of clergy on crusade than we have of computing the total number of noncombatants; but the sources always mention them so as to suggest that they formed no inconsiderable part of the whole. Their presence in large numbers would not be surprising. Pilgrimages to the Holy Land had always attracted them. Religious motives would influence them just as they did pious laymen, and for some clerics material considerations would weigh no less heavily. There was also a horde of restless spirits among the western clergy, who found themselves constrained and chafing under the increasing burden of Cluniac reform, and for whom the crusade would offer a means of escape. The pope probably had no intention of getting rid of turbulent clerics by sending them off on crusade, but his admonitions were not always respected. No bishop could keep watch over the movements of all the clergy in his diocese, and there was little to hinder the departure of priests who were willing to forfeit their posts. For their personal entourages, some of the bishops and leaders, especially those under Cluniac influence, tried to choose only clerics of good character. But others were not always so

careful, and in addition, the crusade army
was not an organized body, in which every
man had to find his place. Thus the monk
weary of his cloister, the restless or adventurous parish priest, the ambitious prelate,
thwarted in some favorite project, or in
disgrace or danger at home, and even an
occasional hermit, all found it pleasant or
expedient to go crusading.

Individual motivation is not easily determined. Piety and an earnest desire for
the success of the crusade were probably
the prime considerations to Adhemar, and
to William, bishop of Orange, who tried
to take up the legate's fallen burden. A
similar enthusiasm seems to have urged
Gerhard, abbot of Allerheiligen in Schaffhausen to take the cross, and led Bonfilius,
bishop of Foligno, in turn reformer, hermit, and saint, to seek the promised land.
Fulcher of Chartres, priest and chronicler,
was inspired by Urban's preaching at Clermont. But a more hysterical fervor must
be ascribed to the priest Etienne of Valence, who conversed in his dreams with
saints and the Saviour, and to the abbot
Baldwin who burned a cross in his fore-
head as a desperate measure to coax money
from the superstitious for his journey. This
spirit, a curious mixture of opportunism,
superstition, and genuine religious feeling,
seems to have animated a large part of the
lower clergy.

Some clerics followed their lords on crusade. The count of Toulouse had several
chaplains with him, of whom his namesake,
Raymond of Agiles, the diligent chronicler
of the holy war, is the most notable. In
the same capacity, Bernard of Valence accompanied the bishop of Puy, a certain
abbot Roger followed Anselm de Ribémonte, one Sannardus attended Robert of
Flanders, and Alexander, amanuensis of
Stephen of Blois, went along to write *cum
summa festinatione* the letters of the faint-
hearted warrior to his Norman princess.

At least two prelates joined the crusade
because despite its perils it seemed safer
than staying at home. Odo, the rebellious
bishop of Bayeux, knew he would find
short shrift in a Normandy pledged to
William Rufus, by whom he had been
driven from England. He joined the forces
of Robert Curthose, but never lived to
reach the Holy Land, dying at Palermo,
where he was buried by Gilbert of Evreux,
the only other Norman bishop participating
in the crusade. It appears that Peter,
saintly bishop of Anagni, was likewise
driven by an unpleasant situation at home
to attach himself to Bohemund's forces.

Ambition ruled Arnulf, chaplain of Robert of Normandy, when he took the cross.
Arnulf was a man of high capability, and
knew it. A scholar of some reputation, he
had taught at Caen, and his pupil, Raoul
of Caen, dedicates his *Gesta Tancredi* to
him in very complimentary terms. He was
noted for his learning, eloquence, and especially his scepticism; for he led the party
opposed to the revelation of the Lance, and
thereby earned himself much opprobrium.
Nevertheless, he appears to have been quite
popular with the common people. Cultivated, sophisticated, at ease with *plebs* and
maiores, of low rank, but outstanding ability, Arnulf did not go on crusade without
the hope of bettering himself. The same is
probably true of his namesake and partisan,
Arnulf, bishop of Martirano, and possibly
of Peter of Narbonne, one of the chief supporters of the count of Toulouse.

No fervent piety led Adalberon, archdeacon of Metz, kinsman of Henry III,
and confidant of the schismatic Henry IV,
to join the crusade. In any case, if Albert's
account may be trusted, none of it was in
evidence when he was caught and killed
by the Turks while playing dice with a
beautiful matron in a grove near Antioch.
Adalberon was hardly unique. And what
except misdirected curiosity induced Otto,
bishop of Strassburg, adherent of the anti-
pope Guibert to join Urban's expedition?
If he had hoped for some material advantage, a change of politics would have been
in order; but he went a schismatic, and
returned, says Bernold, no better than when
he set out. Evidently Otto was not convinced of the holy nature of the crusade.

The passion for relics may have been a factor in drawing to the Levant Gerbault, priest of Lille, who distinguished himself by stealing the precious arm of St George from a hospitable Greek monastery in Asia Minor — a sin for which he received his just deserts. Peter of Narbonne, in his later capacity of archbishop of Apamea, is charged with despoiling the tombs of the patriarchs Abraham, Isaac, and Jacob at Hebron.

A priestly adventurer is portrayed for us by the outraged pen of Anna Comnena. This bellicose cleric fought so fiercely during a skirmish between a crusade squadron and some units of the Byzantine fleet that he evoked from the astonished Greek princess the following prolix but significant comment:

For the rules concerning priests are not the same among the Latins as they are with us; For we are given the command by the canonical laws and teaching of the Gospel, 'Touch not, taste not, handle not! For thou art consecrated.' Whereas the Latin barbarian will simultaneously handle divine things, and wear his shield on his left arm, and hold his spear in his right hand, and at one and the same time he communicates the body and blood of God, and looks murderously and becomes 'a man of blood,' as it says in the psalm of David. For this barbarian race is no less devoted to sacred things than it is to war. And so this man of violence rather than priest wore his priestly garb at the same time that he handled the oar and had an eye equally to naval or land warfare, fighting simultaneously with the sea and with men.

The Western Church had in fact long forbidden priests to bear arms; but this paladin of Christ, confronted by the hated Greek schismatics, refused to be bound by papal decrees, or even by a truce. When he had used up all his darts and stones, 'he discovered a sack of barley-cakes, and began throwing out the barley-cakes from the sack as though they were stones, as if he were officiating and taking a service, and turning war into a sacred celebration.' Disembarking severely wounded, he sought the Greek

leader and embraced him, saying, 'If you had met me on dry land, many of you would have been killed by my hands.' Then he gave the Byzantine captain 'a large silver cup worth one hundred and thirty staters. And with these words and this gift he breathed his last.' There is something here of the same valiant spirit which led Bishop Adhemar to plunge straight into the *mêlée*. If the priesthood included many peasants' sons, it also included many younger sons of the nobility, trained in arms, and burning to make use of them. The crusade must have attracted more than one of this kind.

Subject to the general authority of Bishop Adhemar, the clergy on crusade obeyed his commands with regard to preaching, fasts and processions, and the care of the poor. But both the higher and lower clergy tended to group themselves around the leaders whom they had followed on crusade. They often espoused their masters' quarrels, and looked to them in turn for preferment. These statements are illustrated by some events in the career of Peter of Narbonne. He owed his position as bishop of Albara to Raymond, count of Toulouse, who had besieged and captured the town, and he behaved as one of Raymond's vassals. En route from Marra to Archas, he helped guard the army against surprise attacks, and garrisoned Marra for the count. In keeping with Raymond's best interests, he did his best to prevent the common people, who were clamoring for an immediate march on Jerusalem, from destroying the walls of Marra to hasten the departure. At Jerusalem, Peter held the town of David for Raymond, who obstinately refused to surrender it to Godfrey, the newly-elected Defender of the Holy Sepulchre. Here the bishop served him badly, turning the tower over to Godfrey almost at once; but Raymond's other vassals had refused to help him in the matter at all, as they felt that he was clearly in the wrong.

The clergy were not, however, entirely subservient to the lay power. Peter, for example, displayed his independence strikingly at Marra, where in spite of his careful defense of the count's property, he even acted as spokesman for the rank and file in their demand for the immediate march on Jerusalem. But although they displayed some independence in matters touching the common welfare, the power of the clergy, as opposed to that of the leaders, was small, except when they had the people on their side. This is not surprising. At home the Church had not yet won, and never was fully to win its battle for independence from the secular authority. The defeat of Gregory VII had yet to be retrieved. On crusade the position of the clergy was even weaker, as the emergency conditions and the greater need for armed protection further crippled their ability to stand against the lay power. Their sole attempt to take the reins into their own hands failed completely. Nevertheless, despite some particularist tendencies, the solidarity of the clergy was greater than that of any other group. The sacred character of their office, the mysterious power conferred by ordination, commanded the superstitious respect of all classes, and the moral and intellectual force of the better among them imposed itself even upon the leaders. Consequently, so long as the clergy confined their attention to matters of common concern, to pressing problems such as the care of the poor, discipline, morality, and morale, their influence was strong, and the exercise of their legitimate regulatory functions went unchallenged.

The clergy preached, prayed, confessed the soldiers, gave the last sacraments to the dying, and buried the dead. They celebrated mass regularly, and marriages occasionally — perhaps all too seldom, judging from their constant complaints about the morals of the crusaders. These routine services acquired a new importance on crusade, but much more important were the functions imposed by the perils and hardships of the crusaders' way. Maintenance of morale was vital. In these times of recurrent crisis, the failure to achieve at least a minimum of discipline and cooperation would mean disaster, the destruction of the Christian army; and if the crusade failed, the prestige of the Urbanists would collapse with it. The thoughtful and earnest among the clergy, therefore, had a double responsibility, a duty to both the army and the Church.

From the beginning, the care of the poor was the most difficult task. Never before had such a large host of paupers encumbered an army in the field. It seems impossible to determine what classes entered most prominently into its formation. There is some mention of peasants, but no clue as to their numbers. Perhaps the Italian and Provençal towns had some restless and penniless folk to contribute: the most frequent references to the poor are made by the Provençal chronicler, Raymond of Agiles.

The poor, aged, and infirm who lagged behind Raymond's army were slaughtered like cattle by the wild tribesmen of Sclavonia, who wrested from them their last scanty belongings. They died in droves of famine at Nicaea and Antioch. They were cut off and massacred by the Turks at Marra, and died miserably in a thousand skirmishes and ambushes along the way. What their condition must have been in June, 1098, when the crusaders were pent up in Antioch by the Turks, when many soldiers had lost or eaten their horses, and having sold their arms were reduced to fighting with Turkish weapons, when a noble German knight could no longer live by begging, and had to be fed by scraps from Godfrey's table — this may best be left to the imagination.

In the earlier stages of the crusade, the Emperor Alexius was compelled by self-interest to relieve the situation with alms, first at Constantinople, then across the straits in Asia Minor, and again at Nicaea. But as the crusaders penetrated deeper into Asia Minor, and the poor were deprived of even this inadequate imperial aid, the nobles and clergy had to take over the task.

Raymond of Toulouse distinguished himself by his care for the poor. At Clermont his ambassadors promised aid for indigent crusaders. En route through Sclavonia, he and the bishop of Puy struggled early and late to protect them: the count fought always in the rear to guard the poor stragglers, and was always the last to make camp at night. After the fall of Antioch, Raymond offered to lead the poor, who were failing from hunger and sickness, on a plundering raid into enemy territory; and when he went to besiege Albara, it was with a mass of poor people, and very few knights.

A certain spirit of *noblesse oblige* characterized the attitude of the knights toward the poor. At the siege of Antioch, the leaders set up a fund to replace the horses of knights who lost them. Raymond remarks, 'This fraternal agreement produced very beneficial results; for the poor of our army, who wished to cross the river to gather herbs, feared the frequent attacks of the enemy'; *i.e.*, when the knights no longer feared losing their horses, they were willing to use them in protecting the poor foragers. Raymond also takes pleasure in telling how the poor were permitted to enrich themselves from the spoils after a successful skirmish near Antioch, and ran about joyfully, showing off captured silks, shields, and even horses. In the plundering of a Saracen stronghold on the way to Jerusalem, the looting was conducted in accordance with the wealth of the participants: '. . . our poor, having taken up their booty, began to return, one after the other; thereafter the poor foot-soldiers took the same path, and after them, the men-at-arms.' A nicety of gradation!

Such measures were not enough. The bishop of Puy found it necessary to make strenuous efforts to provide for the poor. The Anonymous, with good reason, calls him the *sustentamentum pauperum;* and even after his death, Peter Bartholomew, who was looking for a vehicle to express his own views, put in the bishop's mouth

characteristic utterances about the duty of the rich to the poor. In his sermons Adhemar used to warn the knights repeatedly:

Not one of you can be saved unless he honors the poor and relieves them. Just as you cannot be saved without them, so can they not live without you. For this reason they must pray with daily supplications for your sins to God, whom you have offended in many ways. Therefore I command that you cherish them for the love of God, and succor them so far as you are able.

Charity, then, was a religious duty; and the clergy therefore preached alms-giving assiduously, and coupled their exhortations with fasts and processions at Antioch and Jerusalem. But this, too, was insufficient. We meet with renewed agitation for the care of the poor soon after the defeat of Kerbogha; and at Archas, early in 1099, poor relief was at last put on a more regular basis — for how long we do not know:

It was preached at this time that the people should give tithes of all they had taken, since there were very many poor and many sick in the army: and it was ordered that they give a fourth part to their priests, whose masses they attended, and a fourth to their bishops. The remaining two parts they were to give to Peter the Hermit, whom they had put in charge of the poor, both lay and clerical.

Peter the Hermit, who was probably a monk, seems to have enjoyed a considerable ascendancy over the rank and file of the army, and was well suited to be treasurer of the poor. It is noteworthy that the clergy had their own poor to relieve, and that they were pressing for a regular income from tithes.

All these measures notwithstanding, the poor underwent extreme suffering and demoralization; and out of their misery and struggle for existence arose the ill-famed band of *Tafurs*, whose exploits have been enlarged upon to form one of the most curious legends of the crusades, but whose historicity may no longer be doubted. Our knowledge of the Tafurs is shadowy, and it is difficult to distinguish fact from fiction concerning them. They probably included only a small part of the poor and unarmed. Guibert of Nogent identifies them with the gypsy-folk or Truands; possibly their nucleus was composed of gypsies, who were very likely to attach themselves to the crusade, and whose organization would be similar to that attributed to the Tafurs. Peter the Hermit's constant association with them, and his influence over them, suggests further that some of the Tafurs may have been left over from the destruction of his band in Asia Minor. But thereafter they appear to have recruited their forces regularly from the poorest among the crusaders.

The Tafurs lived under the rule of a king whom they had chosen for themselves. They camped somewhat apart from the rest of the crusaders, who treated them with a respect born of fear. Incredibly savage and brutalized, they went barefoot and unarmed save for clubs, stones, knives, and variously improvised weapons, and lived by foraging and plunder. Yet they were not entirely devoid of discipline, and Guibert rejects emphatically the suggestion that they were a useless appendage to the army. The crusaders found them ready to carry the heaviest burdens and do the most exhausting labor; and they were doggedly determined in besieging cities, where they acted as slingers, and performed many other tasks besides. They fought in every battle, and distinguished themselves at the storming of Antioch, not only by their bravery in the assault, but by their extreme cruelty in the sack. Upon rare occasions, when other provisions failed, the Tafurs ate human flesh — e.g., at Antioch and Marra, where they consumed portions cut from some of the Saracen dead. Such actions enhanced a reputation for ferocity which it already pleased them to foster, and inspired a wholesome terror among the Turks and native Christians alike. In view of their services in battles and sieges, and their effect upon the morale of the Turks, it would appear that the Tafurs, unlike the bulk of the poor, were an asset to everything except the good name of the crusaders.

Despite the grave problems presented by the poor, no attempt was made until after the fall of Antioch to discourage their participation, if only they were sturdy and capable. The crusaders expected to live in large measure off the country, and it is doubtful that any except the leaders and wealthier knights paid much of their expenses with funds from home. A letter asking for reinforcements, dated October, 1097, expresses marked preference for men of sound body and purse, but takes care to add: '. . . if only you are able to come to us, even with very little, thereafter omnipotent God will provide for you, so that you may live.' The crusaders were too hard up for manpower to refuse any likely recruit, no matter what the state of his finances. This consideration may throw additional light on the efforts of the leaders and clergy to relieve the poor. Religion, pity, and custom probably played the major role in determining their action; but some of them perhaps realized that every man rescued from abject poverty was an addition to the fighting strength of the pilgrim army.

The presence on crusade of large numbers of women, and even children, also caused grave complications. Not all the women were undesirables. A few were noblewomen, more or less suitably escorted, as Urban had urged. Baldwin of Lorraine and Raymond of Toulouse had their wives with them, and so did a few knights. The religious, on the other hand, seem to have been represented among the women by but a single nun, of less than doubtful morality. The rest of the women were probably campfollowers and harlots, of whose activities we have adequate evidence.

The women shared the crusaders' hardships and perils. Several score of them, embarking at Brindisi with the forces of Robert of Normandy and Stephen of Blois, drowned *en masse* when one of the overloaded vessels capsized. At Dorylaeum they braved enemy fire to bring water to the men in the fighting lines — an act for which the Anonymous gives them special commendation. In the exhausting march under the pitiless sun of Asia Minor many died of heat and thirst; Albert describes horrible incidents which he claims to have heard from eye-witnesses. At Marash, in Lesser Armenia, Baldwin's wife Godwera died, worn out by lingering illness. Before Antioch the women died of Saracen arrows and the plague; in Jerusalem a host of them joined in the street-fighting, like the bloody viragoes of the French Revolution.

Far from helpless, the women stood up well under the endless misadventures of the campaign; but the bishops and leaders learned from bitter experience that the army was better off without them. From the siege of Antioch they write with emphasis, 'Let only the men come; for the present leave the women at home!' When the crusaders had routed Kerbogha, Bruno of Lucca, returning from Antioch to his native city, carried the warning that women, as well as paupers, were no longer wanted. But it was too late. The army now had a full complement not only of women and poor, but of incompetents and undesirables of all sorts.

The clergy had the task of preserving elementary order and discipline among this heterogeneous multitude, and of maintaining very modest standards of morality. Describing the situation at Nicaea, Albert remarks: 'It is not to be doubted that along with so many distinguished captains there were present campfollowers of a lower sort: serfs and serving-maids, married and unmarried, and men and women of every station. The bishops, abbots, monks, canons, and priests took charge of these to keep them in order, and keep up their courage.' This was a necessary administrative task, not easy, but probably pleasanter than correcting the morals of the crusaders. The medieval warrior was seldom noted for his chastity, and the clergy could not normally have expected much in the way of conti-

nence from him. But the crusade was a religious expedition, undertaken for the sake of the souls of the participants as well as to free Jerusalem. In times of crisis, then, the question of morality merged with the problem of *morale*. The preaching of the clergy against misconduct in general, and adultery in particular, was directed toward a very important end: to reconcile the soldiers to their Creator; to preserve the sense of righteousness which gave confidence to the Christian army, and in this way, to keep up its fighting spirit.

For this reason it is probable that some movement toward reform was felt after every military reverse; but we have only one instance of really radical action. At the siege of Antioch, which was going very badly, the crusaders began to blame their difficulties upon the iniquitous practices prevalent in the camp. Fulcher says: 'Then, having taken counsel, they cast out the women from the army, married and unmarried, lest perchance, befouled by the mire of riotous living, they might displease God. The women, however, found refuge in the neighboring camps.' One would expect the clergy to have a hand in this measure, which was probably not so sweeping as here represented, and Albert confirms this suspicion. According to his account, the leaders and clergy laid down a reform program: The army was to be purged of all vice and injustice. Prohibitions were renewed against the use of false weights and measures, and cheating of any kind in money-changing or other transactions; steps were taken to prevent thievery, fornication, and adultery. Severe penalties were provided, and judges appointed to apply them. Some persons were chained, some had their heads shaved, others were beaten or branded. As an object-lesson, a man and woman caught in adultery were driven with whips all around the camp. This sounds like an ecclesiastical program, and possibly the judges were priests.

In emergencies the clergy tried to encourage the army more directly. They comforted the soldiers with sermons, masses, fasts, and processions, and often stood right behind them in battle, praying, exhorting, and hearing the last-minute confessions of the fighters. Clad in white garments, holding their crucifixes in their hands, they were a powerful deterrent to panic at Dorylaeum, Antioch, Marra, and Jerusalem. At the Holy City, Arnulf and Peter the Hermit helped close the ranks in preparation for the final assault by allaying the dissensions which had arisen along the way. The bishops and priests never let the people forget why they had undertaken the perilous journey. The death of Adhemar relieved the procrastinating leaders, who were only too happy to linger on the way, of their most powerful corrector; but even so, the rest of the clergy, and the lower clergy in particular, sometimes led, and always seconded the popular demand for a rapid advance to their goal. At Jerusalem, to encourage the assault, the clergy pointed out the place where Christ had suffered and died, and discoursed of the heavenly city which the earthly Jerusalem portended.

It was at Antioch that the clergy made their most striking contribution to morale. There, when the city was closely invested by Kerbogha, and the crusaders were fighting a losing battle with the enemy in the citadel and at the gates, the visions reported by a Lombard priest, and by a French cleric, Etienne Valentin, touched off the series of events which led to the discovery of the Holy Lance, and raised the army from despair to victory. The Lombard clerk set the stage by telling how St Ambrose had appeared to a bishop in Italy, when the crusade had just been launched, and revealed that the papal expedition was indeed divinely inspired, and not merely the result of the *levitas animi* of the French, and promised that the crusaders would take Jerusalem within three years. More than two years, the Lombard pointed out, had now passed, and a turn for the better could soon be expected.

But the common people were still very uneasy, fearing with good reason that the leaders would desert, and leave them to perish. On the night of June 10, 1098, many persons did slip away, laymen and clergy alike; and, says Raymond, if Bohemund and the Bishop of Puy had not closed the gates, very few would have remained. The next day, Etienne Valentin came forward and told his story to the leaders: Christ had appeared to him in the night, and bade him remind the leaders of all that he had done for his people, and admonish them that if they repented of their sins, ceased their fornication with pagan and Christian women, and chanted the response *Congregati sunt* daily, he would send them substantial aid within five days.

This revelation was at first-hand, and promised aid within a brief, definite period. It called for a reform movement, for immediate, healthy action, which would release pent-up emotion, and dispel the apathy and indecision which had fastened themselves upon the army. It not only calmed the spirits and raised the courage of the people, but had the more important effect of forcing the wavering leaders to take a firm stand. That the leaders had any real confidence in Etienne's promise of aid within five days is most unlikely; but his vision expressed the fears and hopes of the multitude, and demanded some gesture to restore their confidence. The bishop of Puy seized his opportunity. While excitement over the revelation was still running high, Adhemar combined clerical with popular pressure to make the leaders swear renewed allegiance to the Christian cause:

. . . the bishop of Puy ordered the Gospels and the Cross to be brought forward, so that he [Etienne] might swear that this thing was true. At that time all our leaders decided that they would swear an oath that none of them would flee, not even if it were a matter of life and death, so long as they were still living. . . . Hearing this oath, the Christian congregation exulted beyond measure.

The connection between Etienne's oath and the oath of the leaders is apparent. Now the *maiores* had to stick it out. This event, more than the discovery of the

Lance, for which it was the necessary preliminary, marked the turning-point, and saved the crusading army.

The Lance at first had less to do with the clergy. Peter Bartholomew was not a priest, or a noncombatant. But Adhemar made as skillful use of the Lance as he had of Etienne's vision. He was in reality cool to Peter from the start; but all doubts and dissensions were carefully smothered until after the defeat of Kerbogha. In the battle, the Lance was carried by the Provençal chronicler, Raymond of Agiles, but in such close proximity to Adhemar that both the Anonymous and Bruno of Lucca, eye-witnesses of the event, made a natural error and credited the bishop with carrying it. This they could scarcely have done if the bishop had made his scepticism known, as indeed he did, later. Adhemar gave the Lance his tacit approval until the crisis was over, in order to maintain the morale of the crusaders. Perhaps he would have continued to pay it deference, if the Provençals had not treated it as private property, and tried to use its prestige for their own advantage.

Not all clerical actions were equally serviceable to the crusade. The quarrel over the Lance brought a sharp cleavage in their ranks, with Arnulf, who led the sceptics, vigorously opposed by the Provençal group, *e.g.*, the bishops of Orange and Agde, Peter of Narbonne, and Raymond of Agiles. The lower clergy tended to split along the same lines. The bishop of Puy could no longer conceal his views. After Adhemar's death, when Arnulf was asked why he doubted, he replied, 'Because the bishop of Puy had doubted,' and none of the opposition ventured to deny it. Instead they manufactured visions to prove that Adhemar was punished in the next world for his scepticism. But as the bishop, with customary moderation, had refused to become a vigorous partisan of either side, the Provençals refrained from besmirching his memory, and were content to have his hair and beard singed a little in Purgatory before assigning him his proper seat in heaven. These dissensions were a source of weakness to the army. By calling forth an overplus of tendentious visions from the seers of the Provençal party, they undermined faith and embittered the relations between the various contingents. These, perhaps, were the quarrels Arnulf tried to appease before Jerusalem; if so, we must credit him with a conciliatory sermon.

A few instances are also recorded in which individual ecclesiastics fell from grace. At Nicaea the pilgrims rescued from the Turks a nun from a convent in Trêves, who had been rash enough to join Peter's expedition. A council of clergy readily forgave her the forced lapse from chastity which she suffered at the hands of the Turks; but she found the forbidden fruit, once tasted, sweeter than the hope of heaven, and fled the camp with her former Saracen captor, now her lover. Adalberon, who has already been mentioned, was no ornament to the church of Metz. Albert records with a trace of satisfaction that the Turks killed him and carried off his lady. Some churchmen, worn out by famine and hardship, fled from the camp at Antioch to the mountains. This withdrawal was justifiable in that a reduction in the number of noncombatants would relieve the strain on the food supply, but it set a bad example. Worse still, there were clerics among the 'rope-dancers,' who slipped down the walls of Antioch and fled, during the night of June 10–11, 1098.

These instances of clerical misbehavior are gratifyingly few, and except for the quarrel over the Lance, unimportant. We hear of no act of desertion among the higher clergy, such as was committed by Stephen of Blois or Hugh of Vermandois. Peter the Hermit fled in a moment of weakness from the siege of Antioch; but he can scarcely be reckoned among the higher clergy, and once he was caught and brought back he returned to his duty and did good service, which is more than can be said for his lay companion in flight, William the Carpenter.

Yet there was good reason for the weaker

spirits to quail. Famine, plague, and Saracen arrows had no respect for holy orders. Death found Roger, chaplain of Anselm de Ribémonte, at *Sparnum castellum,* somewhere in Asia Minor, and the bishop of Russignolo, who had come from Italy with Bohemund, at the camp before Antioch. Ludwig, archdeacon of Toul, and many of his companions, were cut off and massacred by the Turks in the mountains near the same city. Soon after the fall of Antioch, the bishop of Puy, worn out by his endless labors, fell under the shadow of the plague and died, while at Marra the same fate overtook his unofficial successor, William, bishop of Orange. Just before the battle of Ascalon, an Egyptian skirmishing force carried off the bishop of Martirano, who was heard of no more. The plague in the camp before Antioch swept off large numbers of noncombatants, including monks and priests. Albert estimates the dead at one hundred thousand — a pictorial number, literally meaningless, but which indicates that the clergy, too, suffered heavy losses. It is noteworthy that Adhemar had to ordain priests along the way. The Anonymous records this fact in such a way as to suggest that it was a routine function. Raymond of Agiles was elevated to the priesthood while on crusade. Was there a shortage of priests? Not at the outset. The shortage developed en route, and was due to the high mortality rate.

Those of the survivors who chose to remain in the Holy Land might find rare opportunities awaiting them. Within the territory conquered by the crusaders the ecclesiastical situation was greatly confused. The Greek clergy, maintaining a precarious ascendancy, controlled the patriarchates of Antioch and Jerusalem, and held the more important sees, while the Jacobites, Armenians, and Maronites maintained separate church organizations. All the sects suffered grievously during the upheavals attendant upon the crusade. The patriarch of Antioch was savagely tortured by the Turks; the Christians were expelled from Jerusalem, and the Jacobite congregation

had to flee to Egypt. But the Christians were by no means exterminated.

Although not fond of schismatics, the crusaders let the Jacobites, Armenians, and Maronites exercise their religion in peace, presumably for reasons of policy. In the beginning, the Greeks fared even better. The patriarch of Jerusalem associated on terms of intimacy with the papal legate. Differences of rite and usage were forgotten, and a corps of mixed Greek and Latin clerics instated at Antioch. But as relations between the crusaders and the Emperor Alexius grew more and more strained, the Greek position steadily deteriorated. The first ominous note was struck in September, 1098, when the leaders invited Urban to come and help exterminate the heretics, including the Greeks. From this time on the crusaders began to treat the bishoprics of the Holy Land as their property. No important post was given to a Greek cleric. The patriarch of Jerusalem died at Cyprus, and was not to be replaced by one of his countrymen. The patriarch of Antioch, whose demise was not so conveniently timed, found after two years that he could not get along with the Latin churchmen, and left of his own accord. By and large the field was clear for the Latin clergy. If anything, they had more bishoprics than they could either fill or maintain.

Our information is far from complete, but some details may be given concerning the more important sees. When Baldwin and Bohemund made their belated pilgrimage to Jerusalem in 1099, they brought four priests with them — Benedict, Roger, Bartholomew, and Bernard of Valence, the former chaplain of the bishop of Puy. The first was consecrated archbishop of Edessa; the others, bishops of Tarsus, Mamistra, and Artasium respectively. At Antioch, when the Greek patriarch John had withdrawn, the same Bernard took his place. In September, 1098, Raymond of Toulouse presided over the election of Peter of Narbonne as bishop of Albara; Peter later became archbishop of Apamea. In June, 1099, the leaders chose Robert, a priest of Rouen, as bishop of Ramlah, a see rendered especially valuable by the precious remains of St George. They provided for the collection of tithes, and endowed their candidate with gold, silver, and livestock. 'He remained there with joy.' At Jerusalem, canons were assigned to the Holy Sepulchre and the Temple, while Gerhard, abbot of Allerheiligen in Schaffhausen, who had undertaken the long journey for the love of God, was chosen Guardian of the Sepulchre. Even the abbot whom we have noted as burning a false *stigma* on his brow was able to obtain a post, first as abbot of St Mary's in Jehoshaphat, and then as archbishop of Caesarea.

These elections reflected the investiture strife raging in Europe, and would not have met the approval of a Cluniac reformer. Raymond, describing the election of the bishop of Albara, says that the count of Toulouse consulted his chaplains and the other leaders, and then proceeded to choose a bishop. One of the chaplains (perhaps Raymond himself) announced the forthcoming election and inquired if any candidate would present himself. As no one ventured to do so, the clergy and leaders chose Peter of Narbonne, the people assented by acclamation, and the count then invested the bishop with his temporalities. It is clear that the count of Toulouse directed the choice. Similarly, the bishop of Ramlah (Robert of Rouen) seems to have been chosen by the *maiores*.

The richest prize was the patriarchate of Jerusalem. The clergy knew its importance, and wished to elect the spiritual head first, perhaps conceiving that this priority would enable the patriarch to overshadow his secular colleague. One senses a sharp change in their attitude. With peaceful conditions partially restored, they were beginning to shake off their subservience and rise up as at home to challenge the lay power. If Adhemar had lived, their efforts might have succeeded. But they were weakened by the loss of their best leaders, Adhemar and William, bishop of Orange. Save for the bishop of Albara, the right-hand man of the count of Toulouse, they still found it necessary to step softly. Angered by their protests, the leaders proceeded all the more quickly to elect a secular head.

The patriarchate fell to Arnulf of Chocques, chaplain of Robert Curthose. There was some lively electioneering, with the Provençals opposing his election bitterly; but by Raymond's own admission, Arnulf had the majority of the people as well as of the clergy on his side. Arnulf had come up in the world. His rise is an epitome of the extraordinary opportunities the crusade offered to the clergy.

The bishop of Martirano, Arnulf's supporter, obtained the church of Bethlehem, but never lived to rule over the see of Christ's nativity. He was snatched away to an unknown fate by the Turks; and Raymond, who charges that he received the church in return for aiding the election of Arnulf, regards his untimely end as a divine punishment. If we may believe that Arnulf turned out some clergy who held benefices in the Holy Sepulchre, it is quite likely that he undertook to reward his partisans by providing them with places.

The Crusade as a Holy War

J. J. SAUNDERS

J. J. Saunders is a New Zealand historian of the Crusades. Educated at the University of London, he is currently Senior Lecturer in History at the University of Canterbury, Christchurch, N. Z.

O F the three great world-religions, Islam is the only one which was born militant. When Muhammad was driven from his native Mecca to seek refuge in the rival city of Medina, it was not unnatural that he should use the enmity between the two towns to overcome his pagan foes by force. The victory of Islam in Arabia was largely accomplished by the sword, and circumstances induced the Prophet's heirs to employ the armies of tribesmen at their disposal in the propagation of the new faith in the world beyond. The aim of the *jihad*, or holy war, was to enlarge the domain of Islam until the entire globe had been subdued, but this did not imply forcible conversion: on the contrary, the Peoples of the Book (that is, nations with holy scriptures of their own) were to be assured of freedom of worship, and thus under the Caliphs, Christians and Jews all enjoyed toleration.

Buddhism and Christianity, unlike Islam, grew up within the framework of ordered and civilized societies and did not possess the means, even if they had had the will, to conquer the world in the name of their founders. In the days when Rome was still pagan, Christian theologians doubted if a faithful Christian could lawfully serve in an army whose emperor was worshipped as a god; and a strong anti-militarist sentiment pervaded the early Church and even after the conversion of Constantine, St Basil of Cappadocia recommends the soldier who has killed his enemy in war to abstain for three years from holy communion. Yet in face of the example of the Hebrews in the Old Testament, war could not be condemned as immoral *per se*, and St Augustine, in *The City of God*, concedes that it may be waged 'by command of God.' The German scholar Erdmann, in his *Entstehung des Kreuzzügsgedanken* (1935), holds that the early Christians were essentially pacifist, and that militarization came in with the Germans, to whom war was a natural and continual activity: one recalls the story of Clovis, who after listening to a recital of the passion and death of Christ, exclaimed: "Had I been present with my brave Franks, I would have avenged his injuries!" The primitive and barbarous society of the Germanic West was thoroughly war-minded: by contrast the civilized Byzantines treated war as a regrettable necessity, to be avoided as far as possible by diplomacy and other means.

It has often been argued that the Crusading spirit was born in the West in the time of Charlemagne, who was indeed represented in later legend as fighting the Saracens in Palestine: his wars against the pagan Saxons and Avars enlarged the domain of Christendom as well as the Frankish Empire, and the forced baptisms in which he indulged are evidence of a new and startling aggressive type of Christianity. Yet there is a big difference be-

From J. J. Saunders, *Aspects of the Crusades* (Christchurch, New Zealand, 1962), pp. 17–21. Reprinted with permission of the University of Canterbury.

tween Charlemagne's campaigns and the later Crusades. The former were all fought in Europe and could be treated as defensive, as necessary for the protection of Latin Christendom: the latter were unmistakably offensive operations conducted far away across the sea, and (this is the essential point) sponsored and organized by the Church for a purely religious purpose, the recovery of the Holy Places in Palestine.

How did the Latin Church come to adopt war as an instrument of ecclesiastical policy? It has been suggested that, paradoxically, Crusading warfare grew out of the peace movement which the Church had vigorously promoted from the late tenth century onwards in order to check the frightful evils of private war waged, after the collapse of the Carolingian State, by irresponsible and unrestrained feudal lords. Partly out of genuine idealism, partly out of a desire to protect its property in an age of wild licence and political anarchy, the Church set out to mobilize public opinion against lawless brigands in high places: missions were preached, a Truce of God was proclaimed, and crowds were invited to subscribe to a peace oath, the lead being taken by such sovereigns as Robert the Pious in France and the Emperor Henry III in Germany. The results were but meagre: to curb the fighting propensities of feudalism was beyond the Church's power, and clearly the most effective means of putting down the evil would be to come to terms with these turbulent barons and enlist them in campaigns abroad against the enemies of Christendom.

Spain offered a promising field. After the collapse of the Omayyad Caliphate in 1031, Muslim Spain had lapsed into chaos, thus inviting Christian intervention for the recovery of what was after all a lost province of the Latin Church; and in 1063 Pope Alexander II offered an indulgence to all who fought for Christ against the Moors. This brought a crowd of French knights and adventurers streaming across the Pyrenees, and with these powerful reinforcements, Alfonso VI of Castile was able

to capture the old Visigothic capital of Toledo in 1085. The influence of Cluny is discernible here: the reform movement so intimately linked with the great Benedictine abbey in Burgundy had stimulated, among other things, pilgrimages to the shrine of St James at Compostella in Galicia, and the monks of Cluny, if they did not actually organize military expeditions, managed the pilgrim-roads across France into Spain. It was in the inns and hospices along these roads that there grew up the *Chansons de Geste,* which reflected the new spirit of a vigorous if brutal anti-Saracen religious patriotism. We have not yet reached the chivalrous age of Arthur and the Holy Grail: we are still in the barbarized world of the *Song of Roland,* which was in fact the world of the First Crusade.

Yet this Spanish fighting was no true Crusade: the Popes concerned themselves only indirectly with it, and a figure like the Cid, who fought indifferently for Christian or Moor, would have been unthinkable in the Palestine of the next generation. What was needed to bring into being the Holy War proper was that the Popes should proclaim universal peace among Christians and mobilize the faithful in a great offensive against the enemies of the faith, not in Spain or North Africa but in the very cradle of the Christian religion. This could only be done in the peculiar circumstances of the late eleventh century.

First, the great reform movement, which aimed at freeing the Church from the corrupting grip of the feudalized monarchies and lordships, had been driven to look to Rome for leadership and to build up a new conception of papal supremacy. The tremendous conflict over lay investiture between Gregory VII and Henry IV of Germany had underlined this new role of the Papacy and prepared the way for Urban II, in his famous speech at Clermont in 1095, to seize the moral mastery of Europe.

Secondly, the breach between the Greek and Latin Churches, which had been steadily widening, impelled the Hildebrandine Papacy to seek a restoration of Christian unity. We know now, thanks to the work of Runciman and others, that the schism of 1054 was not in fact final and definitive: it came about almost accidentally, and relations between Rome and Constantinople were not wholly broken off. The references in Urban's speech to 'the churches of the East' do hint that a grand reunion of the Christian body was envisaged as a consequence of the defeat of the infidel.

Thirdly, the irruption of the Seljik Turks into Western Asia, which endangered the Byzantine Empire and interrupted the pilgrim traffic to the Holy Land, supplied the final stimulus. The loss to the Turks of central Anatolia, long the chief recruiting-ground of the imperial armies, and the threat to Constantinople itself, drove the Byzantine emperors to seek urgently for reinforcements from the West. The appeal of Michael VII to Pope Gregory in 1073, and of Alexius I to Count Robert of Flanders in 1091 could not go unanswered, and by 1095 it may well have seemed to a shrewd statesman like Urban II an excellent opportunity to achieve at one blow several desirable ends: the relief of the Byzantine Empire from Turkish pressure, the reunion of the Churches, and the rescue of the Holy Places from the enemies of Christ. Given the strong current of religious revivalism then sweeping over the Latin world in the wake of the reform movement, this last would have the strongest appeal.

Thus the Holy War, the very concept of which was unintelligible to the Christian East, was the creation of the reformed Hildebrandine Papacy seeking to make good its bold claims to the overlordship of a united Christendom. It was no conscious imitation of the Muslim *jihad,* for this aimed at *expansion,* whereas the Crusades

aimed at *recovery,* though the notion of fighting for God and the Faith appeared in both. Recent writers, reacting against the tendency of the last generation to ascribe every historic movement to politico-economic motives, have perhaps overstressed the moral and spiritual elements. Thus Paul Alphandery, in his *La Chretiente et l'Idee de Croisade* (1954), sees the Crusade as a genuine expression of popular faith, animated by a kind of collective mysticism and rising up out of an atmosphere of visions, prophecies and miracles, typified by the affair of the Holy Lance at Antioch. Adolf Waas, also, in his *Geschichte der Keruzzüge* (1956), appears to trace its origin to an ideal of dedicated knighthood, of feudal vassalage to God, which goes back to Charlemagne and perhaps even to the pre-Christian society of ancient Germany. This is far-fetched indeed: more prosaically we may say that the Crusades are the outcome of the Latin Church's attempt to tame feudal barbarism and harness it to the service of religion, an attempt which, as we might expect, was only half successful. Swashbuckling scoundrels like Bohemund of Taranto rubbed shoulders with sincere idealists like Godfrey of Bouillon: the saying attributed to the latter, when he was offered the throne of Jerusalem, that he would not wear a crown of gold in the city where his Saviour had worn a crown of thorns, whether authentic or not, remains one of the sublimest phrases of history and reflects the noblest side of the Crusading movement. Certainly the Crusades were the product of a feudal society and could have arisen out of no other: this is why they do not occur in any other age or any other part of Christendom, and this is why the fastidious and peace-loving Byzantines could never see the Frankish soldiers of the Cross as anything but coarse and bloodstained barbarians.

The Crusades and European Expansion

HILMAR C. KRUEGER

Hilmar C. Krueger was born in Milwaukee in 1904. An alumnus of North-western University, he obtained the doctorate at the University of Wisconsin. His research interests have been focused mainly on the economic history of medieval Genoa. He has collaborated in the editing of three important sources for the history of medieval trade, published in the series *Documenti e studi per la storia del commercio e del diritto commerciale italiano* [Documents and Studies for Italian Commercial History and the History of Commercial Law] (Torino, 1939–40). Dr. Krueger is presently Dean of University College at the University of Cincinnati.

THE Crusades were part of a pan-European expansionist movement that pushed into all directions, partially under the impetus or guise of Christianity. The conquest of England by Duke William of Normandy, the foundation of another Norman Kingdom in the Two Sicilies, the Spanish campaigns of the Christian knights of Spain and France, and the Saxon Crusade across the Elbe, the expeditions of the Scandinavian sailors into the northern seas and the Christian settlements in Iceland and Greenland, the acceptance of Roman Christianity by St. Stephen and his Hungarian subjects were all parts of the same expansionist movement, some antecedent, others contemporary, to the more phenomenal overseas expansion. To a great degree this general development made the Crusades possible and acceptable. In all areas the developments continued beyond the end of the twelfth century.

The economic aspects of the Crusades were as varied as the participants. There is little need and no method to weigh and evaluate the varied causes for this overseas expansion. Admittedly, religious, political, and social forces existed in addition to the more material economic factors. Pope Ur-ban II appealed successfully to all interests and by no means did he overlook the economic and material aspects. That these economic interests influenced considerably the activities of some of the crusading elements may be gathered from the denunciations of them when some of the crusades failed to reach the expectations of the more spiritually minded.

In a measure the Crusades were evidence that the Peace of God and the Truce of God had failed. The varied accounts of Pope Urban's speeches refer to bloody strife, plundering and pilfering, homicide and sacrilege, hatreds and dissensions. These actions were economic liabilities for western Europe and any diminution of them was of economic profit to the communities and groups among whom they existed. Urban's references to the actions were couched in terms of religion, humanity, and social conscience, but the economic losses from war and plunder cannot be denied and the gains from their absence cannot be overlooked.

To the feudal barons, "aforetime robbers" who were to become soldiers of Christ, the pope gave promise of material gains. He promised to the overseas crusaders what the bishops and princes of the

From Hilmar C. Krueger, "Economic Aspects of Expanding Europe" in *Twelfth-Century Europe and the Foundations of Modern Society,* ed. Marshall Clagett, Gaines Post and Robert Reynolds (Madison, Wisconsin, 1961), pp. 69–74. Reprinted with permission of University of Wisconsin Press.

north had offered to the Saxon colonists and settlers. "The possessions of the enemy will be yours, too, since you will make spoil of his treasures. . . ." "Wrest that land from the wicked race, and subject it to yourselves, that land which, as the scripture says, 'floweth with milk and honey.'" He obviously hoped to gain the support of the landless or land-poor barony, who possessed little property because of the rules of inheritance or the ill fortune of the feudal wars. He knew, too, the inevitable result of increasing population whose land "is too narrow . . . nor does it abound in wealth; and it furnishes scarcely enough food for its cultivators."

The economic gains that were promised to the feudal barons were also obtained by them. The great princes at the head of their feudal levies carved out the largest estates, but lesser barons established themselves as well. As the crusading armies marched southward from Asia Minor into Syria and Palestine, individual leaders conquered and claimed their personal principalities. In that fashion Tancred established himself in Cilicia, Baldwin in the County of Edessa, and Raymond of Toulouse in the County of Tripoli. They often quarreled with one another in complete disregard of the common cause and the Kingdom of Jerusalem and certainly not in the interests of the Holy Sepulcher and the papal see. With them their own personal ambitions ranked first, and they demanded before anything else the establishment of their own political authority along feudal lines which gave them the customary economic returns in fees, services, fines and products. The lesser barons generally became vassals and enjoyed similar gains, but on a smaller scale. Many of the barons, who had nothing to return to in western Europe, established residence in the Levant and their descendants became part of the Frankish aristocracy of the East. Fulcher of Chartres exclaimed: "He who in Europe owned not so much as a village is lord of a whole city out here. He who was worth no more than a few pence now disposes of a fortune.

Why should we return to the West when we have all we desire here?"

While the feudal barons formed the majority of the fighting men in the crusading campaigns, the Italian townsmen and merchants were so essential to the whole movement that it would have collapsed without their support. After the First Crusade all western armies travelled eastward, by sea, and even in the First Crusade the naval and military support of Genoa and Pisa was considerable. Pope Urban II recognized the importance of the towns and merchants for the movement and accordingly sent itinerant propagandists into the cities to preach the crusades or had local preachers perform the job.

Since the Italian towns had been fighting the Moslems for several centuries, the papal preachers had no difficulty persuading the Italian merchants to coöperate. The Italians had fought the Arabs for three hundred years before 1095, at first defensively, then offensively. All the great Italian cities, Naples, Rome, Pisa, and Genoa in the west, Bari, Ancona, and Venice on the Adriatic, had been attacked and plundered by the Arabs. In the early tenth century the south Italian cities had wiped out the last Arab base in Italy, and in the early eleventh century Genoa and Pisa had driven the Arabs from the Tyrrhenian Sea. In 1087 a combined force of Italian cities, under the leadership of a papal legate, attacked Mehdia in North Africa, plundered a merchant suburb, gained compensation for damages done to their ships by Arab pirates, and obtained free access to the area for their merchants. The victory cleared the western Mediterranean of Arab pirates and competitors. To the Italian cities the call of Pope Urban II sounded like an invitation to help clear the eastern Mediterranean as well and to obtain similar commercial privileges. To the Italian merchants the Crusades always appeared to be extraordinary economic opportunities. From the very start the Italians gained financial rewards. Their ships carried the crusaders and their equipment, even their horses, to the Holy Land, and then supplied the Crusaders with food, drink, and, on occasion, with timber, manpower, and siege machinery. Genoa and Pisa commandeered all possible ships in their domains for transport purposes and ordered the construction of more and larger vessels. The transport services were a source of immediate income for the communes, merchants, and shipowners. The Fourth Crusade is good evidence that financial return loomed large in the aims of the shipowners and merchants. The Crusades gave to the Italian cities much of the liquid capital that was needed in the capitalistic developments that were just beginning. Furthermore, this capital came from sources unrelated to the Italian towns, from western feudal barons and kings. It was money which the Italians could not have obtained otherwise.

In addition to these immediate monetary returns Genoa, Pisa, and Venice received promises of quarters in the coastal towns of Syria and Palestine. These promises were generally made in private agreements between the Italian cities and the baronial leaders, the kings of France and England, and the kings of Jerusalem. Often they were made under pressure of the moment and then forgotten when the pressure was lifted. However, the Italians, especially the Genoese, established themselves well enough to enjoy long-term rewards and profits. In at least a dozen coastal towns of the Levant the Italians possessed throughout most of the twelfth century residential and commercial quarters, from which they gained an income from rentals, leases, harbor dues, and court fines. In these centers the Italian merchants carried on their trade with the European colonists and feudal residents, with Arab traders, and with their associates and agents who worked in the area. The Italian quarters of the Levant became the centers of exchange for Oriental and European goods and markets for the western imports that increased as the century wore on. The Oriental trade was highly profitable and another

source of capital in the new money economy of the period. The Crusades were the strongest influence on the development of medieval trade and industry.

Something needs to be said about the Crusades and the general structure of medieval business and capitalism. First of all, the Crusades created a situation in which capital appeared and circulated. Feudal, clerical, and royal participants mortgaged and sold their holdings to obtain money to buy equipment, hire soldiers, and pay for passage. In some instances they melted down their plate and jewelry. Occasionally, the peasants brought out their hoards and bought their freedom from their anxious and hard-pressed lords. Guibert de Nogent wrote: "As everyone hastened to take the road of God, each hurried to change into money everything that was not of use for the journey, and the price was fixed not by the seller, but by the buyer." Generally, as already indicated, this capital went to the Italian merchants and shippers for transportation or other services connected with the venture. Eventually, numerous other people received jobs and wages, including armorers, shipbuilders, ropemakers, and vintners. Obviously, much of the capital paid to the Italians covered the cost of materials and labor, but a considerable part was profit and gain. In turn, much of the profit was reinvested in the Levantine trade, which also was extremely lucrative. The Crusades had promoted the capitalistic cycle of capital, investment, profit, and reinvestment of profit for further profit and capital. The Crusades, cities, and commerce initiated a money economy which threatened and certainly modified the older land economy of western Europe.

Another capitalistic instrument given impetus by the Crusades was credit. Credit, after all, was based on the expectancy of income and profit by the borrower. Many participants in the Crusades bought their equipment or obtained loans on credit, expecting to profit from the material rewards which Urban had promised. In the Holy Land many again resorted to loans from the Templars and Hospitallers, hoping to repay from their ventures in the Near East or from their properties in western Europe. The rulers, of course, could expect to pay their loans from tax receipts or new crusade aids. The merchants seemingly did less business with the banking orders, partially because they had capital, primarily because they had their own banking systems and credit arrangements. Nevertheless, the Crusades helped to establish credit on an international scale and gave to credit instruments an international operation between the Italian bases in the Levant and the fairs of Champagne and Flanders in the West.

Similarly, the Crusades gave to commerce an international aspect. They again opened up the entire Mediterranean Sea to Christian ships and trade and provided an entry into the trade with the Near and Far East. The crusaders' acquaintance with Arab and Moslem customs created a demand for Oriental goods in Christian Europe, so that dyes, spices, woods, silk, cotton, precious stones, pearls, and alum became regular western imports from the Italian quarters in the East. Henry of Champagne acknowledged some gifts of Saladin with: "You know that your robes and turbans are far from being held in scorn among us. I will certainly wear your gifts." At the same time the growing industries of the West gave the Italian merchants the chance to carry western goods, especially cloths, eastward to exchange them for the Levantine goods, and the continued residence of westerners in the East created a demand for those western wares. While the Italian quarters served as the *entrepot* in the Levant, the fairs of Champagne and Flanders served a similar function in the West. The famous fairs of Troyes, Lagny, Provins, and Bar-sur-Aube were instituted in the twelfth century. But between the two distant points the sea merchants of maritime Italy and the land merchants of North Italy and France carried on a regular cycle of purchases and sales, usually on credit. They thrived on a commerce that had become international. Even though the crusader states and the Kingdom of Jerusalem lost heavily to the Moslems toward the end of the century, the trade relations continued, the coastal cities and the Mediterranean Sea remained open to the European merchants.

The Crusade and the Eastern Question

AZIZ SURYAL ATIYA

Aziz Suryal Atiya was born in Egypt in 1898. Educated in England, he has taught and lectured at many universities in England, Egypt, Germany, and the United States. He has done many specialized studies of the Crusades and Crusading projects in the fourteenth and fifteenth centuries. The best known of Professor Atiya's books are *The Crusades of Nicopolis* (London, 1934), *The Crusades in the Later Middle Ages* (London, 1938), and *Crusade, Commerce and Culture* (Bloomington, Indiana, 1962). Professor Atiya is presently a member of the faculty of the University of Utah.

THE interpretation of the idea of the Crusade has varied from age to age. The medieval thinker regarded it as a holy war for a holy cause directed by the hand of Providence through the offices of the Holy Pontiff — the Vicar of God on earth. Here we sense the Providential view of history prevailing in the Middle Ages. Another medieval interpretation of the Crusade is that it was a pilgrimage or "passagium" conducted to the Holy Places beyond the sea for the remission of sins. The individual pilgrim was known as a "passagium parvum"; whereas a communal or mass pilgrimage in which the participants were fully armed for offensive and defensive purposes was a "passagium generale," that is, a Crusade.

The opposite conception of the Crusade occurred in the time of the Renaissance, as well as in the course of the eighteenth century, when the rationalist philosophers of both eras described this movement as a mere outburst of medieval fanaticism and a demonstration of the bigotry of the medieval mind. These trends found a perfect outlet in Christian aggression against Islam and the Muslim Empire for the deliverance of the birthplace of Christ under the leadership of the Roman See.

The political historian, however, prefers to group the Crusades together as a migratory movement from the West to the East, another kind of "Völkerwanderung," or the wandering of needy nations and tribes in search of terrains more opulent than their own. Were not the Normans and the Franks, the chief initiators of the Crusade, highly famed for their migratory instincts from the dawn of the Middle Ages in the course of the fourth and fifth centuries of our era, the period of the decline and fall of the ancient empire of Rome?

The modern school of economic historians, on the other hand, views the Crusade from a totally different angle as a stage in the eastward expansion of Europe — a form of colonization and of medieval imperialism. During the eleventh century, the population of France and of some adjacent countries is known to have increased all of a sudden beyond the natural output of their meager resources, and it is not inconceivable that these hard-pressed people felt the expediency of exploring new areas for new opportunities. Conscious of the economic difficulties which faced the people, Pope Urban II, in his address of 1095, referred to Palestine as a land where rivers of milk and honey flowed freely. With the progress of the Crusading enterprise and the establishment of the Latin

From Aziz Suryal Atiya, *Crusade, Commerce and Culture* (Bloomington, Indiana, 1962), pp. 17–23. Reprinted with permission of the Indiana University Press.

Kingdom of Jerusalem, a continuous stream of settlers moved from the West to Outremer.

The general consensus of opinion among medievalists, however, is that the Crusades were military expeditions organized by the peoples of Western Christendom, notably the Normans and the French, under the leadership of the Roman Popes, for the recovery of the Holy Places from their Muslim masters. According to the older school of thought, the holy war as such lasted approximately two centuries, from 1095 to 1291 or 1292 A.D. — the lifetime of the Latin kingdom of Jerusalem on the Syrian littoral.

For a comprehensive definition of the Crusade, we have to make a somewhat detailed inquiry into the basic nature of the movement, as well as the circumstances of its realization in a world which it filled with thunder and lightning. In the first place, we must discard the usual treatment of that movement as an entirely separate entity in the annals of mankind. The Crusade should be regarded as one of numerous chapters in the relations between the East and the West. These relations go far back into antiquity beyond the confines of the medieval world. The bone of contention was the undefined frontiers of Europe, otherwise described as the spiritual frontiers of the West vis-a-vis Asia.

In fact it was Greece and the miracle of the Greek mind and Hellenic culture that gave Europe a clear consciousness of its spiritual frontier, which it sought to defend and even extend over the territories east of the Propontic Sea, the modern Marmora. In the fifth century B.C. we begin to perceive unmistakable signs of that marked cleavage between Europe with its Hellenic civilization and Asia as identified with the way of life and thought prevailing in the Persian Empire. This gave birth to what may be described even at that early stage in ancient history as the Eastern Question, that is, the question of the mobile frontiers which separated the realms of Greece and Persia, or, more broadly conceived, Europe and Asia. The rising powers of the future tried to find successive solutions to that standing problem, age after age, from the Greeks to the Romans, the Byzantines, the Carolingians, the Latin Crusaders, and the Muslim Counter-Crusaders. Consequently, we may deduce in all simplicity that the Crusades in their technically limited sense were merely the Frankish Solution of the Eastern Question in medieval times.

In the second place, we must examine the state of medieval Europe and medieval thought in order to be able to evaluate the nature and spontaneity of the Crusade. The Middle Ages were first and foremost an age of faith and of war. These two factors remained continually at work shaping medieval institutions and society and the medieval mind. But nowhere in medieval Europe did these two factors find a fuller expression than in the Crusade — war conducted for a holy cause and fought by the chivalry of Europe and the Church Militant in perfect harmony. The response to Urban II's pronouncements of November 1095 at Clermont-Ferrand in the Auvergne was unanimously *"Deus lo volt!"* God wills it! This was the only comment chivalry had on that memorable occasion. . . .

This call to arms explains the universality of the movement, which may be defined as the contest of the medieval "united nations" of Western Christendom against the forces of all Islam, the apple of discord being Jerusalem and the land of promise, of which the nations of both East and West disputed the right of possession.

The Crusade was initiated as a war of faith and principle on both sides, a duel of words turned into action. The two adversaries did not originally embark on that enterprise in a spirit of self-seeking interest and aggrandizement; and mystical enthusiasts for the cause in the West found their peers in the East in the fields of propaganda and warfare. The careers of Richard the Lion-Heart and the great Saladin have been immortalized by numerous records of their extraordinary feats of chivalry, valor, and honest pursuits. On the other hand, it would be an error to contend that their heroic conduct presented a solitary episode in the annals of the Crusade. The autobiography of Usāmah ibn Munqi*dh* (1095–1188) and the Damascene Chronicle of ibn al-Qalānisī (d. 1160) provide us with innumerable examples showing that the genuine Crusade and the Counter-Crusade almost assumed the shape of daily sport in the borderland of the kingdom of Jerusalem. They were not wars of unmixed malice and treachery, as sordid and as devastating as the wars of Christians among themselves in Europe. Compare the horrors, atrocities, and ravages of the Hundred Years' War between England and France in the later Middle Ages with the local maneuvers between Muslim and Christian princes in the land beyond the sea, and you will ascertain the immense difference in the spirit in which the two conflicts were waged.

Moreover, the Crusade could sometimes paradoxically be presented as an affair of peaceful diplomacy. This approach is exemplified in the relations between Charlemagne and Harūn al-Ra*sh*īd on the eve of the ninth century, Frederick II's encounter with the Aiyubid sultan al-Kāmil in 1229, and the effective exchange of embassies between King James II of Aragon and the Mamluk sultan al-Nāṣir Muhammad ibn Qalāwūn during the first three decades of the fourteenth century.

The Crusade was the Frankish attempt at solving the problem of the Eastern Question in the Middle Ages, whether the means was one of war or one of peace.

ACHIEVEMENTS OF THE CRUSADES

The Crusades: Crowning Glory of the Middle Ages

THOMAS A. ARCHER AND CHARLES L. KINGSFORD

Thomas A. Archer and Charles L. Kingsford were joint authors of *The Crusades: the Story of the Latin Kingdom of Jerusalem*. Their estimate of the achievements of the Crusades reflects the consensus of scholarly opinion at the end of the nineteenth century and the beginning of the twentieth century. Both Archer and Kingsford were Oxford scholars of the last century. Their book on the Crusades was begun originally by Archer alone, but when he was forced by failing health to abandon the project, Kingsford took it over and brought it to completion, re-writing and revising the portions which Archer had completed earlier.

IF the consequences of the Crusades are puzzling in their complexity, no less complex are the motives to which they owed their origin. The enthusiasm of religion, the spirit of adventure, the lust of power, the desire of gain, all, no doubt, contributed in their degree. Probably it is true to say that only of a few Crusaders, as of Godfrey and St. Louis, can we predicate absolute purity of motive. But after all detractions are made, there will still remain the overmastering fact that the Crusades were the outcome of an enthusiasm more deep and enduring than any other that the world has witnessed. They were no mere popular delusion; for principles of sound reason overruled the ungoverned excitement of the mob. No deep-laid plot of papal policy; for neither Gregory VII. when he projected, nor Urban II. when he preached the Holy War, could have foretold the purposes to which their successors would, half unconsciously turn it. Not the savage outbreak of warlike barbarism; for they entailed a patient endurance which only the inspiration of a noble ideal made possible. The Crusades were then primarily wars of an idea, and it is this which sets them apart from all other wars of religion; for into the Crusades proper the spirit of religious intolerance or sectarian jealousy hardly entered. The going on the Crusade was the "Way of God," not to be lightly taken up or lightly laid aside like the common affairs of men. The war was God's warfare, to be waged in His behalf for the recovery of the Heritage of Christ, the land which Our Blessed Lord Himself had trod. If this idea was not present to all when they took the Cross, yet it is safe to say that the great mass of the Crusaders came at some time under its spell. It is hard always for the men of one age to comprehend the enthusiasms of another. We can only marvel at the strange infection which for nearly two centuries ran riot through the West of Europe. It is easier for us to recognise the epic grandeur of the enterprise, in which was concentrated all that was noblest

From Thomas A. Archer and Charles L. Kingsford, *The Crusades* (New York: G. P. Putnam's Sons, 1894), pp. 446–451.

in the mediaeval spirit. The Crusades were the first united effort of Western Christendom. They raised mankind above the ignoble sphere of petty ambitions to seek after an ideal that was neither sordid nor selfish. They called forth all that was most heroic in human nature, and filled the world with the inspiration of noble thoughts and noble deeds. Of the manifold consequences that were to spring from this inspiration, the higher ideals of life, the wider range of understanding, enough has been said already to show that the Crusades were as beneficial in their general results as they were undoubtedly sincere in their original undertaking.

From the consideration of ideals which inspired the Crusaders, we pass naturally to the practical purpose which they endeavoured to achieve. Two principal objects presented themselves to the promoters of the First Crusade. The chief no doubt was the restoration of the Holy Places to Christian rule; the secondary object — but to such leaders at least as Gregory VII. and Urban II. a no less clear one — was the defence of the Eastern Empire against the danger of Turkish conquest. The first was based on a sentiment, but on a sentiment which with some change of form still survives; the second, on an urgent necessity, the pressure of which was yet felt two centuries ago. The first object was within a few years achieved by the establishment of the kingdom of Jerusalem. But the process was barely complete before the process of decay commenced. (With the causes of that decay, the narrow limits and ineffectual frontier of the kingdom, the jealousies of Crusaders for the Syrian Franks and for one another, the rival policies of the military orders and the native baronage, the deterioration of energy amongst those who settled in the East, and the waning enthusiasm amongst those who remained in the West, we have already in their several places dealt.) A failure in this sense the Crusades no doubt were; but with it all we cannot regard as

entirely fruitless an enterprise which maintained a fairly vigorous life for one century, and prolonged its death struggle for another.

The success of the second great object of the Crusades is best regarded from a twofold point of view — firstly, as concerns the Empire of the East; and secondly, as concerns the history of the world at large. In the former case, it seems clear that but for the First Crusade the Empire of the Comneni must have succumbed to the Seljukian Turks. Certainly the twelfth century witnessed a great recovery both of territory and power on the part of the Eastern Empire. But, at the same time, it must be remembered that the constant passage of huge and disorderly hosts was the source of serious harm, and that the destruction of the true Empire of the East was the work of a so-called Crusade. Perhaps it is not too much to say that whatever benefit was wrought by the First Crusade was more than undone by the Fourth. From the time of the latter enterprise there was no strong united power to guard the East, and the success of the Turks was probably due as much to this as to their own prowess. Certainly the political and religious dissensions of East and West were aggravated by the Crusades, but, above all, by the Fourth Crusade, and the power of resistance in Christendom was so far weakened. From this standpoint, therefore, the eventual failure of the Crusades to achieve their second great objective was hardly less complete than it was in the case of the first.

Looking at the Crusades, however, from the more general standpoint of the world's history, we can pass a more favourable judgment. It was an imperative necessity for the welfare of Christendom that the advance of the Turks — which during the eleventh century had made such rapid progress — should be stayed. The First Crusade rolled back the tide of conquest from the walls of Constantinople, and the wars of the next two centuries gave full employment to the superfluous energies of Islam. Even after Acre had fallen, the Latin kingdom of Cyprus, the knights of St. John at Rhodes, and the maritime power of Venice — all creations of the Crusades — combined to delay, if they could not stop, the advance of Mohammedanism. The importance of this for Western civilisation cannot be over-estimated. Had the capture of Constantinople by Mohammed II. been anticipated by three centuries it is impossible that the Turkish conquests should have been confined to the peninsula of the Balkans and the valley of the Lower Danube. A new influx of barbarism, at the very moment when the gloom of the Dark Ages was breaking, might have been as ruinous to the social and political life of Western Europe as it was to that of Western Asia. At the least it must have put back the progress of civilisation in Europe by centuries, if it had not altered utterly the course of the world's history. . . .

It is easy to contrast the glories of the Renaissance with the wreck of Mediaevalism, and to feel that between the two there is a great gulf fixed. But the mediaeval world had had its own glories, which, as they faded, let fall the seeds of future prosperity. The processes of decay and new birth are as natural to the historical as to the physical world, and there is no justice in the taunt of failure; for it is in the failures and half-successes of one age that there are sown the seeds of the glories of another. The Middle Ages were, in their way, as important and fruitful for mankind as any other epoch of the world's history. The Crusades were their crowning glory of political achievement, the central drama to which all other incidents were in some degree subordinate. If the enthusiasm which produced them perished, it was not until it had borne good fruit: we may perhaps contrast the age of the Crusades with the age of the Early Renaissance, which succeeded it, in some respects to the disadvantage of the former; but when all is said and written this much at least must be admitted: it was not altogether a change from the worse to the better that gave France a Louis the Treacherous for a Louis the Saint, and England a Richard of the Subtle Brain for a Richard of the Lion Heart.

The Crusades: A Military Failure

ARNOLD J. TOYNBEE

Arnold J. Toynbee was born in 1889 and was educated at Winchester and Balliol College, Oxford. He is Director of Studies at the Royal Institute of International Affairs and Professor at the University of London. His *Study of History* is an attempt to classify and interpret the whole of human history in terms of the civilizations which men have created for themselves, and to deduce from the histories of past civilizations the prospects of man's future.

IF we ask ourselves why it was that a Medieval Western Christendom's lasting gains of territory from the Crusades amounted only to such disproportionately small returns for so gigantic an expenditure of effort, we shall find more than one answer to our question.

One obvious explanation of the ultimate defeat of the Crusades lies in the excessive dispersion of the Western aggressors' energies. They attacked their neighbours on no less than five fronts — in the Iberian Peninsula, in South Italy, in the Balkan Peninsula, in Syria, and in the Continental European borderland between Western Christendom and Russia — and it is not surprising that they should have failed to obtain any decisive results from this improvident use of a limited fund of surplus Western energy which might have carried their offensive forward to some permanently tenable 'natural frontier' if it had been concentrated steadily on any single front out of the five.

If the French Crusaders, for example, had concentrated their efforts on reinforcing an Iberian front that lay at France's doors, Western Christendom might have reached the natural frontier of the Sahara, not in the twentieth century, but in the thirteenth, instead of halting for a quarter of a millennium — from the fifth decade of the thirteenth century to A.D. 1492 — at the foothills of the Sierra Nevada and then for more than four centuries thereafter at the straits of Gibraltar, which in all previous ages had been a bridge and not a barrier between the Iberian Peninsula and the Maghrib. The impetus of Western Christian aggression against the Maghribī province of Dār-al-Islām was weakened by the division of Western Christian forces between an Iberian and an Apulian front; yet, even so, if the Normans who headed for Apulia instead of Leon had concentrated thenceforward on this single new enterprise, they might perhaps still have reached a Saharan natural frontier on this Central Mediterranean front likewise, via Sicily and Tunisia. Instead, they dispersed their energies once again by invading the Transadriatic dominions of the East Roman Empire in A.D. 1081 before they had completed their conquest of Sicily, and then riding off on the First Crusade to carve out a Syrian principality for themselves round Antioch. Thereafter, when the Normans did tardily embark on the conquest of Ifrīqīyah in A.D. 1134, they allowed themselves to be diverted from carrying this African enterprise through to completion by being drawn into a great war with the East Roman Empire (*gerebatur* A.D. 1147–56) which was as exhausting as it was inconclusive.

The Levantine front that was opened

From *A Study of History*, Volume VIII, by Arnold J. Toynbee. Oxford University Press, 1954, pp. 357–363. Reprinted by permission.

up in the First Crusade had to compete
with the demands of the already active
fronts in the Central and the Western Mediterranean, yet the residue of Western
Christian military effort that could be mo-
bilized for action in Syria might still perhaps have sufficed to establish a tenable
frontier in this distant theatre of operations
if the Crusaders had been prudent enough
to refrain from straying across the Euphrates and resolute enough to push forward
to the fringe of the North Arabian Steppe
all along the line from the right bank of
the Euphrates to the head of the Gulf of
Aqabah. They did succeed in reaching this
natural frontier at its southern end, and
thereby momentarily insulating Cairo from
Damascus, and Mecca from both, by plant-
ing outposts of the Kingdom of Jerusalem
at Aylah and Karak; but these strategically
momentous acquisitions remained as precarious as they were provocative so long
as the left flank of the Western intruders'
Transjordanian salient remained open to
counter-attack from Dār-al-Islām's vast un-
conquered Asiatic interior. This deadly gap
in the defences of the Terre d'Outre Mer
could have been closed at the outset by
the leaders of the First Crusade if, instead
of crossing the Euphrates to seize an un-
tenable Edessa, they had expended an
equal amount of energy on occupying the
key position of Aleppo between Antioch
and the Syrian bank of the Euphrates and
on securing all the crossings of the Euphrates between the southern spurs of the
Antitaurus and the northern fringe of the
North Arabian Steppe; for, had they thus
sealed Syria off at the northern end, as
they afterwards duly sealed it off at the
southern end by occupying Karak and
Aqabah, they could then have reduced
Hamah, Homs, and Damascus at their
leisure; and this strategy would have driven
between a Sunnī Muslim Caliphate in Irāq
and a Shī'ī Muslim Anticaliphate in Egypt
a wedge of Frankish territory that might
have been proof against any Muslim blow
that could have been struck at it from
either side.

In the event, the Crusaders' neglect of
the natural frontier offered by the elbow
of the Euphrates was to deliver them into
the hands of a rejuvenated Sunnī Muslim
Power which the challenge of the Crusades called into existence. This new
Power's first base of operations was Irāq,
whose irrigation-system, which was the
source of its agricultural productivity, had
not yet been wrecked by Mongol barbarian
invaders; and the first in the series of war-
rior-statesmen who built this Power up was
Zengī (dominabatur A.D. 1127–46), who
was appointed in A.D. 1127 by the Saljūq
Imperial Government to be atābeg (count)
of the metropolitan province of a shrunken
Abbasid Caliphate which the Saljūqs had
liberated from the domination of the Shī'ī
Buwayhids in A.D. 1055. Within a year
of his installation at Baghdad, Zengī won
for himself a dominion of his own by annexing Mosul and the Jazīrah; and he
immediately followed up these conquests
on the east side of the Euphrates by crossing the river and releasing the stalwart
outpost city of Aleppo from its encirclement by the Frankish principalities of
Edessa and Antioch. Edessa, now encir-
cled in its turn, fell to Zengī in A.D. 1144;
Zengī's son and successor Nūr-ad-Dīn
(dominabatur A.D. 1146–74) was able to
hold his ground west of the Euphrates
against the Second Crusade (gerebatur
A.D. 1146–9), and Nūr-ad-Dīn's subse-
quent annexation of Damascus in A.D.
1154 provided his lieutenant Shīrkūh and
Shīrkūh's nephew, colleague, and successor, Saladin, with a base of operations for
breaking through the screen of Frankish
outposts between Karak and 'Aqabah in
order to compete with Amalric, King of
Jerusalem, for the conquest of Egypt from
a decrepit Fātimid Shī'ī régime.

Three successive pairs of rival expeditions (gesta A.D. 1163–4, 1167, 1168–9)
ended in Egypt's remaining in Saladin's
hands. The Western intruders' Terre
d'Outre Mer then found itself enveloped
by its Sunnī Muslim adversaries, and this
encirclement spelled the doom of the

Frankish Power in Syria; but Saladin was too good a strategist to strike before he had consolidated his now commanding position. In A.D. 1171 he extinguished the Fātimid Anticaliphate and restored *de jure* the sovereignty of an 'Abbasid Caliphate at Baghdad over an Egypt whose resources were at Saladin's own disposal *de facto.* Thereafter he rounded off his empire by first annexing Tripolitania, the Eastern Sudan, and the Yaman (A.D. 1172–4) and then, after the death of his overlord Nūr-ad-Dīn, making himself master of everything between the eastern borders of the Frankish principalities in Syria and the western foothills of the Zagros in Kurdistan (A.D. 1174–86). When he struck at the Franks at last in A.D. 1187 the result was a foregone conclusion. The Third Crusade could not save the Terre d'Outre Mer from being reduced to a few bridgeheads along the Syrian coast.

The characteristically short-sighted counter-move of the leaders of the Fourth Crusade to Saladin's conclusive defeat of the Third Crusade in Syria was, as we have seen, to commit a now hard-pressed Western Christendom to yet a fourth Mediterranean front in the domain of the East Roman Empire; and here the disastrous effects of the Western aggressors' persistent dispersion of their energies made themselves felt more signally and more swiftly than in any other theatre. A Frankish host that was strong enough to deal the East Roman Empire an irretrievable blow by storming and sacking its sacrosanct and hitherto impregnable capital had not the strength to seize more than a handful of the fragments into which the shattered empire broke up, and even these meagre pickings slipped, one by one, out of the covetous Frankish hand that had clutched them. A Monferratine 'Kingdom of Salonica' lasted no longer than eighteen years (A.D. 1204–22) and a French 'empire' at Constantinople no longer than fifty-seven (A.D. 1204–61), while the French Principality of the Morea melted away less rapidly, but not less inexorably, from A.D.

1262 onwards. The Italian city-states alone showed a capacity for retaining and increasing their share of the spoils that the Fourth Crusade had picked up from the wreckage of a wantonly shattered East Roman Empire.

A second explanation of the failure of the Crusades is to be found in the disappointment of the Crusaders' fond hope that a heaven-sent 'Prester John' would miraculously redress in Christendom's favour a balance which Saladin's genius had inclined so heavily to the advantage of the Crusaders' Muslim adversaries. In the event, the Mongol world-conquerors did not become converts to a Christianity of either the Roman or the Nestorian persuasion. The Roman Catholic archbishopric that was founded in A.D. 1294 by John of Montecorvino in the Mongol Khāqān's southern capital at Khanbalyq (Peking), on the inner side of the Great Wall, expired in the course of the fourteenth century as obscurely as the Norse settlements in Greenland. The prize of converting the last still pagan Eurasian Nomads was eventually divided between Islam and the Tantric Mahayanian Buddhism of Tibet, and in the thirteenth, fourteenth, and fifteenth centuries Islam found other new worlds besides to conquer in Yunnan, the Deccan, Indonesia, the Sudan, Western Anatolia, and Rumelia.

The event thus exposed the vanity of a thirteenth-century Western Christian dream that Islam might be stamped out by an enveloping centripetal reflux of the western and eastern arcs of a Christian wave which had previously been receding centrifugally in all directions under the pressure of a following Islamic wave's advance. The visionary thirteenth-century Western observers who had dreamed this dream had not been mistaken in their intuition that, in the domain of Islam on which the Crusaders were trespassing, a mighty institution was passing away; their mistake had lain in identifying this moribund institution with the religion that had been revealed to Mankind through the

Prophet Muhammad. The institution that was actually *in extremis* in the thirteenth century of the Christian Era was a Syriac Civilization whose disintegration had been retarded by an intrusion of Hellenism and whose universal state, originally embodied in the Achaemenian Empire, had been reestablished by the Muslim Arab empire-builders a thousand years after the destruction of the Achaemenian Empire by Alexander the Great.

Islam might indeed have died out if it had never outgrown its original function of providing a distinctive heretical religious badge for Arab war-bands that had accidentally reconstituted a Syriac universal state in the shape of the Caliphate as a by-product of the barbarian successor-state that they had been bent on carving out of the Roman Empire. It would in fact have died out if the Umayyads, like their Visigothic contemporaries and victims, had elected to abandon their distinctive barbarian heresy in favour of their Christian subjects' orthodoxy. In that event the *ci-devant* Muslim Umayyad Arab conquerors of Syria would have become converts to the Monophysite form of Christianity, like their predecessors the *ci-devant* pagan Ghassanid Arab wardens of the Roman Empire's Syrian desert marches. This possibility had passed away when the replacement of the Umayyad dynasty by the Abbasids had transferred the ascendancy in the Caliphate from the Arabs to their Khurāsānī clients and had substituted the profession of Islam for the possession of an Arab pedigree as the qualification for membership in a dominant minority. From that time onwards the spiritual gifts and intellectual abilities of all peoples in a politically reunited Syriac World had contributed to build Islam up into an oecumenical higher religion which could compete with Christianity on the strength of the elements that it had borrowed from it; and, in the next and last chapter of Syriac history, this enriched Islam had begun to make mass-conversions among a now dissolving Caliphate's Christian and Zoroastrian subjects, not only by virtue of its intrinsic spiritual merits, but for the sake of the enduring social order which Islam promised to provide for a world that was appalled at the prospect of losing the oecumenical framework which had hitherto been provided for it by the political institution of the Caliphate.

The future of Islam had thus been assured before an already tottering Baghdādī Abbasid Caliphate finally succumbed to a *coup de grâce* from the Mongols. So far from threatening Islam with destruction, the invasions of the Caliphate's derelict domain by the Crusaders from one side and by the Mongols from the other were the finishing touches in the making of Islam's fortune; for, when the Baghdādī Abbasid Caliphate foundered, and all that was left of the old fabric of Syriac society went down with it, Islam did not die, but lived on to offer refuge to the shipwrecked children of a lost civilization. Islam not only captivated the savage Mongol conquerors of the Caliphate; she served as a chrysalis for bringing to birth two new societies to take the place of a Syriac society that had finally dissolved in the post-Abbasid interregnum; and the emergence of the Iranic and Arabic Muslim civilizations set the seal on the discomfiture of the Western Christian Crusaders.

In the first place these nascent societies, in the vigour of their early youth, created war machines with which the Crusaders could not compete. In another context we have taken note of the overthrow of Saint Louis' disorderly knights by a trained and disciplined Egyptian Mamlūk cavalry at Mansūrah in A.D. 1250. The still better trained and disciplined Ottoman Janissary infantry, which overthrew the Mamlūks in A.D. 1516–17, had the upper hand over their Western Christian adversaries from the fourteenth century to the seventeenth, when their military ascendancy was tardily wrested from them by Western troops who conquered them by at last successfully imitating them. But sheer military superiority was not the whole explanation of the two new-born Islamic civilizations' triumph over the West; for the Iranic Muslim Civilization, at any rate, gained the day by its superior attractiveness as much as by its superior strength. When, in the fourteenth and fifteenth centuries, Greek Orthodox Christians who could no longer look forward to remaining their own masters found themselves still free to choose between a Frankish and an Ottoman domination, they opted for the Osmanlis; and a minority among them that was willing to contract out of an onerous political servitude by abandoning a traditional religious allegiance showed less repugnance towards becoming converts to Islam than toward staying within the Christian fold at the price of becoming ecclesiastical subjects of the Pope. While the Greeks' historic choice was partly determined by the negative motive of resentment at the overbearing behaviour by which the Franks had made themselves odious in Greek eyes, some credit must also be given to the positive attraction exerted by the Ottoman way of life, in view of the significant fact that, in the golden age of Ottoman history, the Christian renegades who 'turned Turk' were not exclusively Orthodox Christians who had found themselves caught between an Ottoman and a Frankish mill-stone, but were also recruited from among Western Christians who were not under any corresponding pressure to change their religious allegiance against their inclinations.

In spite of the strength and attractiveness of the Osmanlis, the Franks might perhaps have retained permanent possession of at least a remnant of their acquisitions in the former domain of the East Roman Empire if the late Medieval Western cosmos of city-states, of which the North and Central Italian city-states were the foremost representatives, had succeeded in assimilating to itself the relatively backward feudal mass of a Medieval Western Christian body social. The Italians were condemned by an inexorable fiat of geography to live and move and have their being in the Mediterranean; they had invested heavily in commerce and sovereignty in the Levant; and, though they were at least as unpopular as the French, Catalan, and Navarrese Franks among Orthodox Christians who could not avoid encountering them, they were at any rate more efficient than their Transalpine and Transmarine coreligionists — as was demonstrated by the accumulation in Venetian, Genoese, and Florentine hands of an ever increasing proportion of the constantly diminishing Frankish assets in the Levant in the course of the thirteenth, fourteenth, and fifteenth centuries.

If the Italian city-states had been backed by a Western World in which their own order of society had prevailed, they might perhaps have proved strong enough with this solid support in their rear to save the situation for Western Christendom on its Mediterranean Front; but, as we have noticed in another context, the ninth decade of the fourteenth century saw the end of any prospect that the Western World as a whole might find its way to modernization through a mass-conversion to the city-state dispensation which had made the fortunes of the precociously modern Italians and Flemings. In the event, the feudal mass of a Medieval Western Christendom modernized itself, not by remitting its kingdoms into city-states, but by adapting to the kingdom-state scale of political operations the efficient administrative apparatus which late medieval North Italian despots had imported from the East Roman Empire via its Sicilian successor-state; and the Modern Western World that was actually called into existence crystallized, not round the Mediterranean city-states of Italy, but round the Atlantic kingdoms and commonwealths of Portugal, Spain, France, England, and Holland. A Venice, Genoa, and Florence that had thus lost their lead within their native Western Christendom had, *a fortiori*, lost their chance of heading a united Western resistance to the progress of the Osmanlis in the Levant, while the Atlantic countries that had won the lead and acquired the power were too eagerly preoccupied with the conquest of the Ocean to be willing to spend much energy on stemming the Osmanlis' advance in a Mediterranean that had dwindled into being a backwater.

These considerations, between them, perhaps go some way towards accounting for the Crusaders' eventual failure. Our findings may be summed up in the verdict that the Medieval Western Christian competitors for dominion over the Mediterranean Basin were neither strong enough to subdue their neighbours nor cultivated enough to captivate them.

The Crusades: A Moral Failure

SIR STEVEN RUNCIMAN

Sir Steven Runciman was born in 1903. He was educated at Eton and at Trinity College, Cambridge. He has taught at Cambridge, the University of Istanbul, Oxford, and St. Andrew's, as well as serving in the English diplomatic service. He has written extensively in Byzantine history and one of his major works is a monumental *History of the Crusades*. He was knighted in 1958.

THE Crusades were launched to save Eastern Christendom from the Moslems. When they ended the whole of Eastern Christendom was under Moslem rule. When Pope Urban preached his great sermon at Clermont the Turks seemed about to threaten the Bosphorus. When Pope Pius II preached the last Crusade the Turks were crossing the Danube. Of the last fruits of the movement, Rhodes fell to the Turks in 1523, and Cyprus, ruined by its wars with Egypt and Genoa and annexed at last by Venice, passed to them in 1570. All that was left to the conquerors from the West was a handful of Greek islands that Venice continued precariously to hold. The Turkish advance was checked not by any concerted effort of Christendom but by the action of the states most nearly concerned, Venice and the Hapsburg Empire, with France, the old protagonist in the Holy War, persistently supporting the infidel. The Ottoman Empire began to decline through its own failure to maintain an efficient government for its great possessions, till it could no longer oppose the ambition of its neighbours nor crush the nationalist spirit of its Christian subjects, preserved by those Churches whose independence the Crusaders had tried so hard to destroy.

Seen in the perspective of history the whole Crusading movement was a vast fiasco. The almost miraculous success of the First Crusade set up Frankish states in Outremer; and a century later, when all seemed lost, the gallant effort of the Third Crusade preserved them for another hundred years. But the tenuous kingdom of Jerusalem and its sister principalities were a puny outcome from so much energy and enthusiasm. For three centuries there was hardly a potentate in Europe who did not at some time vow with fervour to go on the Holy War. There was not a country that failed to send soldiers to fight for Christendom in the East. Jerusalem was in the mind of every man and woman. Yet the efforts to hold or to recapture the Holy City were peculiarly capricious and inept. Nor did these efforts have the effect on the general history of the Western Europeans that might have been expected from them. The era of the Crusades is one of the most important in the history of Western civilization. When it began, western Europe was only just emerging from the long period of barbarian invasions that we call the Dark Ages. When it ended, that great burgeoning that we call the Renaissance had just begun. But we cannot assign any direct part in this development to the Crusaders themselves. The Crusades had nothing to do with the new security in the West, which enabled merchants and scholars to travel as they pleased. There was already access to the stored-up learning of the Moslem world through

From Sir Steven Runciman, *A History of the Crusades* (Cambridge, England, 1951–58), pp. 469–480. Reprinted by permission of Cambridge University Press.

Spain; students, such as Gerbert of Aurillac, had already visited the Spanish centres of education. Throughout the Crusading period itself, it was Sicily rather than the lands of Outremer that provided a meeting-place for Arab, Greek and Western culture. Intellectually, Outremer added next to nothing. It was possible for a man of the calibre of Saint Louis to spend several years there without the slightest effect on his cultural outlook. If the Emperor Frederick II took an interest in Oriental civilization, that was due to his upbringing in Sicily. Nor did Outremer contribute to the progress of Western art, except in the realm of military architecture and, perhaps, in the introduction of the pointed arch. In the art of warfare, apart from castle-building, the West showed again and again that it learned nothing from the Crusades. The same mistakes were made by every expedition from the First Crusade to the Crusade of Nicopolis. The circumstances of warfare in the East differed so greatly from those in Western Europe that it was only the knights resident in Outremer who troubled to remember past experience. It is possible that the general standard of living in the West was raised by the desire of returning soldiers and pilgrims to copy the comforts of Outremer in their homelands. But the commerce between East and West, though it was increased by the Crusades, did not depend on them for its existence.

It was only in some aspects of the political development of western Europe that the Crusades left a mark. One of Pope Urban's expressed aims in preaching the Crusades was to find some useful work for the turbulent and bellicose barons who otherwise spent their energy on civil wars at home; and the removal of large sections of that unruly element to the East undoubtedly helped the rise of monarchical power in the West, to the ultimate detriment of the Papacy. But meanwhile the Papacy itself benefited. The Pope had launched the Crusade as an international Christian movement under his leadership; and its initial success greatly enhanced his power and prestige. The Crusaders all belonged to his flock. Their conquests were his conquests. As, one by one, the ancient Patriarchates of Antioch, Jerusalem and Constantinople fell under his dominion, it seemed that his claim to be the Head of Christendom was justified. In Church affairs his dominion was vastly extended. Congregations in every part of the Christian world acknowledged his spiritual supremacy. His missionaries travelled as far afield as Ethiopia and China. The whole movement stimulated the organization of the Papal Chancery on a far more international basis than before, and it played a great part in the development of Canon Law. Had the Popes been content to reap ecclesiastical benefits alone, they would have had good cause for self-congratulation. But the times were not yet ready for a clear division between ecclesiastical and lay politics; and in lay politics the Papacy overreached itself. The Crusade commanded respect only when it was directed against the infidel. The Fourth Crusade, directed, if not preached, against the Christians of the East, was followed by a Crusade against the heretics of southern France and the nobles that showed them sympathy; and this was succeeded by Crusades preached against the Hohenstaufen; till at last the Crusade came to mean any war against the enemies of Papal policy, and all the spiritual paraphernalia of indulgences and heavenly rewards was used to support the lay ambitions of the Papal See. The triumph of the Popes in ruining the Emperors both of the East and of the West led them on into the humiliations of the Sicilian war and the captivity at Avignon. The Holy War was warped to become a tragic farce.

Apart from the widening of the spiritual dominion of Rome, the chief benefit obtained by Western Christendom from the Crusades was negative. When they began, the main seats of civilization were in the East, at Constantinople and at Cairo. When they ended, civilization had moved its headquarters to Italy and the young countries of the West. The Crusades were not the only cause for the decline of the Moslem world. The invasions of the Turks had already undermined the Abbasid Caliphate of Baghdad and even without the Crusade they might ultimately have brought down the Fatimid Caliphate of Egypt. But had it not been for the incessant irritation of the wars against the Franks, the Turks might well have been integrated into the Arab world and provided for it a new vitality and strength without destroying its basic unity. The Mongol invasions were more destructive still to Arab civilization, and their coming cannot be blamed on the Crusades. But had it not been for the Crusades the Arabs would have been far better able to meet the Mongol aggression. The intrusive Frankish State was a festering sore that the Moslems could never forget. So long as it distracted them they could never wholly concentrate on other problems.

But the real harm done to Islam by the Crusades was subtler. The Islamic State was a theocracy whose political welfare depended on the Caliphate, the line of priest-kings to whom custom had given a hereditary succession. The Crusading attack came when the Abbasid Caliphate was unable politically or geographically to lead Islam against it; and the Fatimid Caliphs, as heretics, could not command a wide enough allegiance. The leaders who arose to defeat the Christians, men like Nur ed-Din and Saladin, were heroic figures who were given respect and devotion, but they were adventurers. The Ayubites, for all their ability, could never be accepted as the supreme rulers of Islam, because they were not Caliphs; they were not even descended from the Prophet. They had no proper place in the theocracy of Islam. The Mongol destruction of Baghdad in some way eased the Moslem task. The Mameluks were able to found a durable state in Egypt because there was no longer a lawful Caliphate in Baghdad, but only a shadowy and spurious line that was kept in honourable confinement in Cairo. The Ottoman Sultans eventually solved the problem by assuming the Caliphate themselves. Their immense power made the Moslem world accept them, but never wholeheartedly; for they too were usurpers and not of the prophet's line. Christianity allowed from the outset a distinction between the things that are Caesar's and the things that are God's; and so, when the medieval conception of the undivided political City of God broke down, its vitality was unimpaired. But Islam was conceived as a political and religious unity. This unity had been cracked before the Crusades; but the events of those centuries made the cracks too wide to be mended. The great Ottoman Sultans achieved a superficial repair, but only for a time. The cracks have endured to this day.

Even more harmful was the effect of the Holy War on the spirit of Islam. Any religion that is based on an exclusive Revelation is bound to show some contempt for the unbeliever. But Islam was not intolerant in its early days. Mahomet himself considered that Jews and Christians had received a partial Revelation and were therefore not to be persecuted. Under the early Caliphs the Christians played an honourable part in Arab society. A remarkably large number of the early Arabic thinkers and writers were Christians, who provided a useful intellectual stimulus; for the Moslems, with their reliance on the Word of God, given once and for all time in the Koran, tended to remain static and unenterprising in their thought. Nor was the rivalry of the Caliphate with Christian Byzantium entirely unfriendly. Scholars and technicians passed too and fro between the two Empires to their mutual benefit. The Holy War begun by the Franks ruined these good relations. The savage intolerance shown by the Crusaders was answered by growing intolerance amongst the Moslems. The broad humanity of Saladin and his family were soon to be rare among their fellow-believers. By the time of the Mameluks, the Moslems were as narrow as the Franks. Their Christian subjects were amongst the first to suffer from it. They never recovered their old easy acquaintanceship with their Moslem neighbours and masters. Their own intellectual life faded away, and with it the widening influence that it had upon Islam. Except in Persia, with its own disquieting heretic traditions, the Moslems enclosed themselves behind the curtain of their faith; and an intolerant faith is incapable of progress.

The harm done by the Crusades to Islam was small in comparison with that done by them to Eastern Christendom. Pope Urban II had bidden the Crusaders go forth that the Christians of the East might be helped and rescued. It was a strange rescue; for when the work was over, Eastern Christendom lay under infidel domination and the Crusaders themselves had done all that they could to prevent its recovery. When they set themselves up in the East they treated their Christian subjects no better than the Caliph had done before them. Indeed, they were sterner, for they interfered in the religious practices of the local churches. When they were ejected they left the local Christians unprotected to bear the wrath of the Moslem conquerors. It is true that the native Christians themselves earned a fuller measure of this wrath by their desperate belief that the Mongols would give them the lasting freedom that they had not obtained from the Franks. Their penalty was severe and complete. Weighed down by cruel restrictions and humiliations they dwindled into unimportance. Even their land was punished. The lovely Syrian coastline was ravaged and left desolate. The Holy City itself sank neglected into a long, untranquil decline.

The tragedy of the Syrian Christians was incidental to the failure of the Crusades; but the destruction of Byzantium was the result of deliberate malice. The real disaster of the Crusades was the inability of Western Christendom to comprehend Byzantium. Throughout the ages there have always been hopeful politicians who believe that if only the peoples of the world could come closer together they would love and understand each other. It is a tragic delusion. So long as Byzantium and the West

had little to do with each other their relations were friendly. Western pilgrims and soldiers of fortune were welcomed in the imperial city and went home to tell of its splendours; but there were not enough of them to make friction. There were occasional bones of contention between the Byzantine Emperor and the Western Powers; but either the bone was dropped in time or some tactful formula for its division was devised. There were constant religious issues, exacerbated by the claims of the Hildebrandine Papacy. But even there, with good-will on both sides, some working arrangement could have been made. But with the Norman determination to expand into the Eastern Mediterranean a new disquieting era began. Byzantine interests were flung into sharp conflict with those of a Western people. The Normans were checked, and the Crusades were launched as a peace-making move. But there was misunderstanding from the outset. The Emperor thought that it was his Christian duty to restore his frontiers to be a bulwark against the Turks, whom he considered to be the enemy. The Crusaders wished to push on to the Holy Land. They had come to fight the Holy War against the infidels of every race. While their leaders failed to appreciate the Emperor's policy, thousands of soldiers and pilgrims found themselves in a land where the language, the customs and the religion seemed to them strange and incomprehensible and therefore wrong. They expected the peasants and citizens in the territory through which they passed not only to resemble them but also to welcome them. They were doubly disappointed. Quite failing to realize that their thieving and destructive habits could not win them the affection or the respect of their victims, they were hurt, angry and envious. Had it been left to the choice of the ordinary Crusading soldier Constantinople would have been attacked and sacked at a far earlier date. But the leaders of the Crusade were at first too conscious of their Christian duty and restrained their followers. Louis VII refused to accept the advice of some of his nobles and bishops to take arms against the Christian city; and though Frederick Barbarossa toyed with the idea, he controlled his anger and passed by. It was left to the greedy cynics that directed the Fourth Crusade to take advantage of a momentary weakness in the Byzantine state to plot and achieve its destruction.

The Latin Empire of Constantinople, conceived in sin, was a puny child for whose welfare the West eagerly sacrificed the needs of its children in the Holy Land. The Popes themselves were far more anxious to keep the unwilling Greeks under their ecclesiastical rule than to rescue Jerusalem. When the Byzantines recovered their capital Western pontiffs and politicians alike worked hard to restore Western control. The Crusade had become a movement not for the protection of Christendom but for the establishment of the authority of the Roman Church.

The determination of the Westerners to conquer and colonize the lands of Byzantium was disastrous for the interests of Outremer. It was more disastrous still for European civilization. Constantinople was still the centre of the civilized Christian world. In the pages of Villehardouin we see reflected the impression that it made on the knights that had come from France and Italy to conquer it. They could not believe that so superb a city could exist on earth; it was of all cities the sovereign. Like most barbarian invaders, the men of the Fourth Crusade did not intend to destroy what they found. They meant to share in it and dominate it. But their greed and their clumsiness led them to indulge in irreparable destruction. Only the Venetians, with their higher level of culture, knew what it would be most profitable to save. Italy, indeed, reaped some benefit from the decline and fall of Byzantium. The Frankish settlers in Byzantine lands, though they brought a superficial and romantic vitality to the hills and valleys of Greece, were unfitted to understand the long Greek tradition of culture. But the Italians, whose connections with Greece had never been broken for

long, were better able to appreciate the value of what they took; and when the decline of Byzantium meant the dispersal of its scholars, they found a welcome in Italy. The spread of humanism in Italy was an indirect result of the Fourth Crusade.

The Italian Renaissance is a matter of pride for mankind. But it would have been better could it have been achieved without the ruin of Eastern Christendom. Byzantine culture survived the shock of the Fourth Crusade. In the fourteenth and early fifteenth centuries Byzantine art and thought flowered in splendid profusion. But the political basis of the Empire was insecure. Indeed, since 1204 it was no longer an Empire but one state amongst many others as strong or stronger. Faced with the hostility of the West and the rivalry of its Balkan neighbours, it could no longer guard Christendom against the Turks. It was the Crusaders themselves who wilfully broke down the defence of Christendom and thus allowed the infidel to cross the Straits and penetrate into the heart of Europe. The true martyrs of the Crusade were not the gallant knights who fell fighting at the Horns of Hattin or before the towers of Acre, but the innocent Christians of the Balkans, as well as of Anatolia and Syria, who were handed over to persecution and slavery.

To the Crusaders themselves their failures were inexplicable. They were fighting for the cause of the Almighty; and if faith and logic were correct, that cause should have triumphed. In the first flush of success, they entitled their chronicles the *Gesta Dei per Francos,* God's work done by the hand of the Franks. But after the First Crusade there followed a long train of disasters; and even the victories of the Third Crusade were incomplete and unsure. There were evil forces about which thwarted God's work. At first the blame could be lain in Byzantium, on the schismatic Emperor and his ungodly people who refused to recognize the divine mission of the Crusaders. But after the Fourth Crusade that excuse could no longer be maintained; yet things went steadily worse. Moralist preachers might claim that God was angry with His warriors because of their sins. There was some truth in this, but as complete explanation it collapsed when Saint Louis led his army into one of the greatest disasters that the Crusaders ever underwent; for Saint Louis was a man whom the medieval world believed to be without sin. In fact it was not so much wickedness as stupidity that ruined the Holy Wars. Yet such is human nature that a man will admit far more readily to being a sinner than a fool. No one amongst the Crusaders would admit that their real crimes were a wilful and narrow ignorance and an irresponsible lack of foresight.

The chief motive that impelled the Christian armies eastward was faith. But the sincerity and simplicity of their faith led them into pitfalls. It carried them through incredible hardships to victory on the First Crusade, whose success seemed miraculous. The Crusaders therefore expected that miracles would continue to save them when difficulties arose. Their confidence made them foolhardy; and even to the end, at Nicopolis as at Antioch, they were certain that they would receive divine support. Again, their faith by its very simplicity made them intolerant. Their God was a jealous God; they could never conceive it possible that the God of Islam might be the same Power. The colonists settled in Outremer might reach a wider view; but the soldiers from the West came to fight for the Christian God; and to them anyone who showed tolerance to the infidel was a traitor. Even those that worshipped the Christian God in a different ritual were suspect and deplored.

This genuine faith was often combined with unashamed greed. Few Christians have ever thought it incongruous to combine God's work with the acquisition of material advantages. That the soldiers of God should extract territory and wealth from the infidel was right. It was justifiable to rob the heretic and the schismatic also.

Worldly ambitions helped to produce the gallant adventurousness on which much of the early success of the movement was based. But greed and the lust for power are dangerous masters. They breed impatience; for man's life is short and he needs quick results. They breed jealousy and disloyalty; for offices and possessions are limited, and it is impossible to satisfy every claimant. There was a constant feud between the Franks already established in the East and those that came out to fight the infidel and to seek their fortune. Each saw the war from a different point of view. In the turmoil of envy, distrust and intrigue, few campaigns had much chance of success. Quarrels and inefficiency were enhanced by ignorance. The colonists slowly adapted themselves to the ways and the climate of the Levant; they began to learn how their enemies fought and how to make friends with them. But the newly-come Crusader found himself in an utterly unfamiliar world, and he was usually too proud to admit his limitations. He disliked his cousins of Outremer and would not listen to them. So expedition after expedition made the same mistakes and reached the same sorry end.

Powerful and intelligent leadership might have saved the movement. But the feudal background from which the Crusaders were drawn made it difficult for a leader to be accepted. The Crusades were the Pope's work; but Papal Legates were seldom good generals. There were many able men amongst the Kings of Jerusalem; but they had little authority over their own subjects and none over their visiting allies. The Military Orders, who provided the finest and most experienced soldiers, were independent and jealous of each other. National armies led by a King seemed at one time to offer a better weapon; but though Richard of England, who was a soldier of genius, was one of the few successful commanders amongst the Crusaders, the other royal expeditions were without exception disastrous. It was difficult for any monarch to go campaigning for long in lands so far from his own. Coeur-de-Lion's and Saint Louis's sojourns in the East were made at the expense of the welfare of England and France. The financial cost, in particular, was appallingly high. The Italian cities could make the Crusades a profitable affair; and independent nobles who hoped to found estates or marry heiresses in Outremer might find their outlay returned. But to send the royal army overseas was a costly undertaking with very little hope of material recompense. Special taxes must be raised throughout the kingdom. It was not surprising that practical-minded kings, such as Philip IV of France, preferred to raise the taxes and then stay at home. The ideal leader, a great soldier and diplomat, with time and money to spend in the East and a wide understanding of Eastern ways, was never to be found. It was indeed less remarkable that the Crusading movement faded away in failure than that it should ever have met with success, and that, with scarcely one victory to its credit after its spectacular foundation, Outremer should have lasted for two hundred years.

The triumphs of the Crusade were the triumphs of faith. But faith without wisdom is a dangerous thing. By the inexorable laws of history the whole world pays for the crimes and follies of each of its citizens. In the long sequence of interaction and fusion between Orient and Occident out of which our civilization has grown, the Crusades were a tragic and destructive episode. The historian as he gazes back across the centuries at their gallant story must find his admiration overcast by sorrow at the witness that it bears to the limitations of human nature. There was so much courage and so little honour, so much devotion and so little understanding. High ideals were besmirched by cruelty and greed, enterprise and endurance by a blind and narrow self-righteousness; and the Holy War itself was nothing more than a long act of intolerance in the name of God, which is the sin against the Holy Ghost.

The Crusades: The Victory of Barbarism

EDWARD GIBBON

. . . As soon as the arms of the Franks were withdrawn, the impression, though not the memory, was erased in the Mahometan realms of Egypt and Syria. The faithful disciples of the prophet were never tempted by a profane desire to study the laws or language of the idolaters; nor did the simplicity of their primitive manners receive the slightest alteration from their intercourse in peace and war with the unknown strangers of the West. The Greeks, who thought themselves proud, but who were only vain, shewed a disposition somewhat less inflexible. In the efforts for the recovery of their empire they emulated the valour, discipline, and tactics of their antagonists. The modern literature of the West they might justly despise; but its free spirit would instruct them in the rights of man; and some institutions of public and private life were adopted from the French. The correspondence of Constantinople and Italy diffused the knowledge of the Latin tongue; and several of the fathers and classics were at length honoured with a Greek version. But the national and religious prejudices of the Orientals were inflamed by persecution; and the reign of the Latins confirmed the separation of the two churches.

If we compare, at the era of the crusades, the Latins of Europe with the Greeks and Arabians, their respective degrees of knowledge, industry and art, our rude ancestors must be content with the third rank in the scale of nations. Their successive improvement and present superiority may be ascribed to a peculiar energy of character, to an active and imitative spirit, unknown to their more polished rivals, who at that time were in a stationary or retrograde state. With such a disposition, the Latins should have derived the most early and essential benefits from a series of events which opened to their eyes the prospect of the world, and introduced them to a long and frequent intercourse with the more cultivated regions of the East. The first and most obvious progress was in trade and manufactures, in the arts which are strongly prompted by the thirst of wealth, the calls of necessity, and the gratification of the sense of vanity. Among the crowd of unthinking fanatics, a captive or a pilgrim might sometimes observe the superior refinements of Cairo and Constantinople: the first importer of windmills was the benefactor of nations; and, if such blessings are enjoyed without any grateful remembrance, history has condescended to notice the more apparent luxuries of silk and sugar, which were transported into Italy from Greece and Egypt. But the intellectual wants of the Latins were more slowly felt and supplied; the ardour of studious curiosity was awakened in Europe by different causes and more recent events; and, in the age of the crusades, they viewed with careless indifference the literature of the Greeks and Arabians. Some rudiments of mathematical and medicinal knowledge might be imparted in practice and in figures; necessity might produce some interpreters for the grosser business of merchants and soldiers; but the commerce of the Orientals had not diffused the study and knowledge of their languages in the schools of Europe. If a similar principle of religion repulsed the idiom of the Koran, it should have excited their patience and curiosity to

From Edward Gibbon, *The Decline and Fall of the Roman Empire,* Vol. VI, ed. J. B. Bury (London, 1898), pp. 442–446.

understand the original text of the gospel; and the same grammar would have unfolded the sense of Plato and the beauties of Homer. Yet in a reign of sixty years, the Latins of Constantinople disdained the speech and learning of their subjects; and the manuscripts were the only treasures which the natives might enjoy without rapine or envy. Aristotle was indeed the oracle of the Western universities; but it was a barbarous Aristotle; and, instead of ascending to the fountain-head, his Latin votaries humbly accepted a corrupt and remote version from the Jews and Moors of Andalusia. The principle of the crusades was a savage fanaticism; and the most important effects were analogous to the cause. Each pilgrim was ambitious to return with his sacred spoils, the relics of Greece and Palestine; and each relic was preceded and followed by a train of miracles and visions. The belief of the Catholics was corrupted by new legends, their practice by new superstitions; and the establishment of the inquisition, the mendicant orders of monks and friars, the last abuse of indulgences, and the final progress of idolatry, flowed from the baleful fountain of the holy war. The active spirit of the Latins preyed on the vitals of their reason and religion; and, if the ninth and tenth centuries were the times of darkness, the thirteenth and fourteenth were the age of absurdity and fable.

In the profession of Christianity, in the cultivation of a fertile land, the northern conquerors of the Roman empire insensibly mingled with the provincials and rekindled the embers of the arts of antiquity. Their settlements about the age of Charlemagne had acquired some degree of order and stability, when they were overwhelmed by new swarms of invaders, the Normans, Saracens, and Hungarians, who replunged the western countries of Europe into their former state of anarchy and barbarism. About the eleventh century, the second tempest had subsided by the expulsion or conversion of the enemies of Christendom: the tide of civilisation, which had so long ebbed, began to flow with a steady and accelerated course; and a fairer prospect was opened to the hopes and efforts of the rising generations. Great was the success, and rapid the progress, during the two hundred years of the crusades; and some philosophers have applauded the propitious influence of these holy wars, which appear to me to have checked, rather than forwarded, the maturity of Europe. The lives and labours of missions, which were buried in the East, would have been more profitably employed in the improvement of their native country: the accumulated stock of industry and wealth would have overflowed in navigation and trade; and the Latins would have been enriched and enlightened by a pure and friendly correspondence with the climates of the East. In one respect I can indeed perceive the accidental operation of the crusades, not so much in producing a benefit, as in removing an evil. The larger portion of the inhabitants of Europe was chained to the soil, without freedom, or property, or knowledge; and the two orders of ecclesiastics and nobles, whose numbers were comparatively small, alone deserved the name of citizens and men. This oppressive system was supported by the arts of the clergy and the swords of the barons. The authority of the priests operated in the darker ages as a salutary antidote: they prevented the total extinction of letters, mitigated the fierceness of the times, sheltered the poor and defenceless, and preserved or revived the peace and order of civil society. But the independence, rapine, and discord of the feudal lords were unmixed with any semblance of good; and every hope of industry and improvement was crushed by the iron weight of the martial aristocracy. Among the causes that undermined the Gothic edifice, a conspicuous place must be allowed to the crusades. The estates of the barons were dissipated, and their race was often extinguished, in the costly and perilous expeditions. Their poverty extorted from their pride those charters of freedom which unlocked the fetters of the slave, secured the farm of the peasant and the shop of the artificer, and gradually restored a substance and a soul to the most numerous and useful part of the community. The conflagration which destroyed the tall and barren trees of the forest gave air and scope to the vegetation of the smaller and nutritive plants of the soil.

The Crusades: The Victory of Idealism

LOUIS BRÉHIER

During the period of a thousand years which comprises what is usually called "the middle ages," the situation of the Eastern nations never ceased to attract the attention of the popes and of the whole church. At the end of the ancient period, the East was the vital sector of the civilized world. Everyone who was eager for learning turned to the East: it was from the East that theologians, monastic reformers, and artists sought their inspiration. It was by passing through the East that the unsophisticated faithful were able to come in contact with the remnants of biblical or gospel history, which, so to speak, came to life before their eyes in the names of even the most modest towns. During this fertile period from the fourth to the seventh century there developed in the West a fad for journeys to the Holy Places and a curiosity about things oriental.

This is what explains the fact that the ruin of the Christian communities of the East aroused the pity of the westerners at the spectacle of the misfortunes which struck their eastern brethren. Once he had become the temporal leader of the West, Charlemagne established a protectorate over the Christians of Palestine — a protectorate which lasted longer than his dynasty itself and which for two centuries made pilgrimages to the Holy Land feasible. In this way, when the short-lived persecution by al-Ḥākim in the ninth century and then the misunderstanding which resulted in the Greek schism and finally the Turkish invasion made the route to Palestine quite dangerous, westerners could not make up their minds to abandon Palestine, but began instead to form groups in order to make the sacred journey. It was this enthusiasm for the veneration of the Holy Sepulchre and, at the same time, this acquaintance with things oriental which caused the Crusading movement. When, following the church reform movement and the investiture struggle, the popes became aware of their political power, they dreamed of using it to defend the Christian East against the Turkish advance and, at the same time, of introducing through this diversionary movement greater order and discipline into feudal society. Gregory VII and Alexius Comnenus wanted to bring together western forces for the defence of the Byzantine Empire. To Urban II belongs the idea of the Crusade. The Emperor of Constantinople sought help from the pope: Urban II replied by a mass rising of Christendom against the Muslim world.

The first Crusades resulted in the foundation of the Latin states in the East as a common patrimony of the faithful, owing their organization to the efforts of French knights while their wealth was exploited from an early period by the maritime cities of Italy. From that time onward, the defence and enlargement of the territories of the Latin East became the supreme goal of the political activity of the popes and, on several occasions, the greatest sovereigns of Europe — the Emperor, the King of France, the King of England — had to abandon their immediate interests to go to the defence of the Holy Land. Such results, however, could be achieved only by great effort and under the emotional pressure generated by some famous Muslim victory. Actually, after the twelfth century there develops an antagonism between the popes' generous actions on behalf of Pales-

From Louis Bréhier, *L'Église et L'Orient au moyen âge: les Croisades,* 2nd Edition (Paris, 1907), pp. 348–355. Reprinted with permission of Librairie Victor Lecoffre. [Editor's Translation]

tine and the temporal politics of the nations, which are eager for tangible results. Surrounded by enemies and weakened by the rowdiness of their own constitutive elements, the Latin states were soon left to their own devices and could rely only on the all-too-interested help of the Italian cities. If, from time to time, they arouse the interest of kings, it was because of their wealth. Thus we see the Hohenstaufens, Henry VI and Frederick II, attempt to secure control of the East for their own profit. The struggle between the empire and the papacy was carried in this way into the Holy Land and the diversion of the Crusade of 1204 to Constantinople was the first serious reversal suffered by papal policy. While it was defended by Western help, the Byzantine Empire had been able to reform itself and to recover its historical role at the frontiers of European civilization. The Latin Empire, on the other hand, far from being able to assist in the defence of Christendom, was only a source of weakness and embarrassment. This was the period in which the forces necessary for the Crusade began to be dissipated in all kinds of enterprises: there were Crusaders fighting in Spain against the Moors, in the south of France against the Albigensians, in Prussia against the northern pagans, in England against John Lackland, in Germany against Frederick II. Soon there were Crusaders everywhere except in Palestine. The idea of the Crusade emerged from this crisis thoroughly discredited. Even the terrible invasion by the Mongols could not tear the European states away from their own quarrels. The example of St. Louis, who united a full awareness of the interests of his own kingdom with a consciousness of the needs of Christian unity, was a unique one. Europe abandoned her eastern colonies to their own fate and viewed the fall of Jerusalem in 1244, of Constantinople in 1261, and of St. Jean d'Acre in 1291 without reaction.

At the same time, while the ideal of the Crusade was dwindling in this way, the relationship of Christendom to the East was taking on a new form and the followers of St. Francis of Assisi and of St. Dominic were beginning their missions to the unbelievers. The sudden contact which brought European Christendom and the civilizations of the Far East together following the Mongol invasions opened an unlimited field to missionary activity. At first the popes hoped to profit from the Mongols' beneficent attitude toward the Christians by concluding an alliance with them against Islam. These diplomatic approaches, however, were not followed through adequately and the indifference of the westerners blocked the attempts made by the Mongols to wrest Syria from Egyptian domination. The fourteenth century is for the relations between Church and the East (as in other fields) a period of confused activity during which Europe seemed to be groping its way. There is a considerable disparity between the abundance of plans, of missions, and of Crusades which are conceived in this period and the insignificant attempts made to carry them out. It was no help when the piratical attacks of Muslim corsairs and the advances made by the Ottomans caused the Venetians to lend assistance to the pope by organizing a flotilla whose numerical inferiority made it useless. A thirst for romantic adventures inspired the expeditions of Peter of Cyprus, of Boucicaut, and of the knights of Nicopolis, but this was not sufficient to make up for the lack of discipline which led western knights to ignominious defeat. As if these disasters were not enough, the end of the fourteenth century and the beginning of the fifteenth were marked by new catastrophes. The missions in China, so prosperous under Mongol domination, were destroyed by the national uprising which brought the Ming dynasty to power. In Central Asia the Mongols were freely converted to Islam and, although the diversionary activities of Timurlane might check momentarily the power of the Ottomans, the westerners were not able to profit from this episode by re-establishing a foothold in the East. Europe, divided against itself, absorbed in the struggles of the great schism, the Hundred Years War, and the Crusade against the Hussites, was an almost indifferent witness to the agonies of the Byzantine Empire. Under Eugene IV, the papacy made a supreme effort to shake off this listlessness, but neither the union of Florence nor the Crusade of Varna could save Constantinople. The events of 1453 brought the Turks to live in Europe, just as the capture of Jerusalem in 1244 had the result of turning Egypt and Syria over to the Mamluks. While they continued to preach the Crusade, the popes had to accept the *modus vivendi* which allowed the Christians of Syria to live, as they had before the Crusades, under Muslim domination. This state of affairs was at first considered a provisional one, but as it came to be guaranteed by the great powers (particularly France, which was the first to do so), it became the definitive state of relations between the church and the East.

The Christians of Syria were thus put back under a Frankish protectorate, as they had been before the Crusades. In the face of this negative result, people have often been tempted to regard as sterile the struggles carried on for five hundred years by Christendom against Islam. Must one conclude, then, that the Crusades had no historical significance and that they succeeded only in squandering the forces of Europe in a total loss? It is too often forgotten that the Crusade began as a defensive war and that, whatever the inconveniences which may have resulted from it, the Byzantine Empire received from the Crusade an effective protection against the Turks at the end of the eleventh century. Islam never ceased expanding up to the end of the twelfth century. Thereafter it had to fight for existence — and fight on its own ground. If in the fourteenth century Islam resumed its onward march, this happened only after the

enthusiasm for the Crusade had died down.

Such, then, are the direct results in the East of the actions of the popes at a period when Europe was divided up into feudal states and when the popes alone understood the menace of Islam's progress for Christian civilization. But perhaps even more important are the results which the popes never dreamed of and which stem indirectly from the relationship of Christendom with the East. The complex question of the borrowings by European civilization from the East cannot be raised here. Every day, however, we discover new traces of the attraction which Eastern culture held for Europeans, whether before or after the Crusades. What seems to us even more important is the increase in geographical knowledge and, at the same time, the extension of European civilization which resulted from these expeditions and journeys into the East. Asia was truly discovered in the thirteenth century by the missionaries and the Italian merchants who were the guests of the Mongol khans. For the first time since Alexander's expedition these regions, which up to now had remained in the shadow of legends, were seen as realities. Thus it is just to place John of Plano Carpini, William Rubrouck, Marco Polo, John of Monte Corvino, Oderico de Pordenone, and many others among the predecessors of Christopher Columbus and Vasco da Gama. Moreover, the *conquistadores* themselves were fired by the spirit of the Crusade and, while searching for new worlds, they never abandoned the idea of finding possible allies against the Saracens and of working at the task of propagating Christianity. It would be unjust to condemn out of hand these five centuries of heroism which had such fertile results for the history of Europe and which left behind in the consciences of modern peoples a certain ideal of generosity and a taste for sacrifice in behalf of noble causes which the harshest lessons of reality will never erase completely.

SUGGESTIONS FOR ADDITIONAL READING

The history of the Crusades has been a perennially popular topic for historical investigators and writers. Consequently the literature dealing with the Crusades is vast and extensive. The most comprehensive bibliography of Crusading history is Hans Eberhard Mayer's *Bibliographie zur Geschichte der Kreuzzüge* (Hannover, 1960), which lists more than five thousand books and articles. There is also a recent and useful introduction to the bibliography of the Crusades by A. S. Atiya, *The Crusades: Historiography and Bibliography* (Bloomington, Ind., 1962). Atiya's bibliography is much less comprehensive than Mayer's, but beginning students may find it easier to use.

The most ambitious effort to deal with the history of the whole Crusading movement in recent times is the cooperative *History of the Crusades,* published by the University of Pennsylvania under the general editorship of Kenneth M. Setton (Philadelphia, 1955–   ). Two volumes of the five which are planned in the cooperative *History* have appeared thus far. Volume 1 deals with the first hundred years of the Crusades, down to 1189. Volume 2 deals with the period 1189–1311. Each chapter in these volumes is the work of a scholar who has specialized in the study of the particular segment of the period under review. Thus volume 1 of the cooperative *History* was written by sixteen different authors; twenty-one authors collaborated to produce volume 2.

The most readable general history of the Crusades in English is the three-volume *History of the Crusades* (Cambridge, 1951–54) by the distinguished Byzantine historian, Sir Steven Runciman. There is also an extensive three-volume history of the movement in French by the orientalist, René Grousset, under the title *Histoire des croisades et du royaume Franc de Jérusalem* (Paris, 1934–36).

There are several short accounts of the Crusades in English. Sir Ernest Barker's little book *The Crusades* (London, 1939), is a slightly revised and extended version of his article in the 1912 edition of the *Encyclopaedia Britannica*. Richard A. Newhall's *The Crusades* is another short history, originally published in 1927 and reissued with some minor revisions in 1963. A. S. Atiya's *Crusade, Commerce and Culture* (Bloomington, Ind., 1962) is an interpretative essay on the Crusading movement written by a well-known Egyptian scholar. There is also a short narrative history by James A. Brundage, entitled *The Crusades: A Documentary Survey* (Milwaukee, 1962). This book combines a brief survey of the movement with translations of a number of the pertinent documents, many of which are not elsewhere available in English.

The best history of the Crusader states available in English is still Dana Carleton Munro's *Kingdom of the Crusaders* (New York, 1936). There is a more recent work in French on the Latin Kingdom of Jerusalem by Jean Richard, *Le royaume latin de Jérusalem* (Paris, 1953). A detailed study of the government of the Latin Kingdom is presented by John L. LaMonte in his *Feudal Monarchy in the Latin Kingdom of Jerusalem* (Cambridge, Mass., 1932).

Many important narratives and documents relating to the history of the Crusades are still not available in English. A collection of the most important sources may be found in the *Recueil des historiens des croisades* (16 vols.; Paris, 1841–1906), published under the sponsorship of the Académie des Inscriptions et Belles-Lettres. The *Recueil* presents the texts of the sources in the original languages: Latin, French, Greek, Arabic, and Armenian. French translations are also given for the texts in Greek and the oriental languages.

Since the Second World War the Académie des Inscriptions et Belles-Lettres has begun to issue a supplementary series of Crusading documents under the title *Documents relatifs à l'histoire des croisades* (Paris, 1946–   ). Many other narratives and documents relating to the Crusades are to be found, as well, in the other great published collections of medieval source materials. Guides to these series and to the Crusading documents which they contain may be found in the bibliographies by Mayer and by Atiya, listed above.

Fortunately for English-speaking students, an increasing number of the source accounts of the Crusading expeditions are being translated into English. The fourteen volumes of the Palestine Pilgrims' Text Society's *Publications* (London, 1896–1907) provide translations of many narratives of interest for the history of the Crusades. A. C. Krey's *The First Crusade* (Princeton, 1921) provides translations of the more important narrative sources for the expedition of 1095–99. Translations of a number of Crusading texts, too, have been published in Columbia University's *Records of Civilization* series. This series includes translations of William of Tyre's *History of Deeds Done Beyond the Sea* by E. A. Babcock and A. C. Krey (2 vols.; New York, 1943); of the *De expugnatione Lyxbonensi*, dealing with the second Crusade, by C. W. David (New York, 1936); of the *De profectione Ludovici VII in orientem* of Odo of Deuil, which also deals with the second Crusade, by Virginia G. Berry (New York, 1948); of Ambroise's *The Crusade of Richard Lion-Heart*, dealing with the third Crusade, by M. J.

Hubert and John L. LaMonte (New York, 1941); of *The Wars of Frederick II Against the Ibelins*, which deals with the Crusade of 1227–29, by John L. LaMonte and M. J. Hubert (New York, 1936); of Robert de Clari's *Conquest of Constantinople*, dealing with the fourth Crusade, by E. H. McNeal (New York, 1936); and the memoirs of Usamah ibn Munqidh, translated under the title of *An Arab-Syrian Gentleman and Warrior in the Period of the Crusades* by P. K. Hitti (New York, 1929). Other translations of significant sources may be found in the *Makers of Christendom* series, which includes a volume of documents concerning the thirteenth century attempts to enlist the Mongols in the Crusading effort (*The Mongol Mission,* ed. by Christopher Dawson, New York, 1955) and a fine translation of Jean de Joinville's *Life of St. Louis* by René Hague (New York, 1955). Another translation of Joinville, together with a translation of Geoffrey de Villehardouin's account of *The Conquest of Constantinople* may be found in *Memoirs of the Crusades* by Sir Frank Marzials. An important source for the first Crusade is the *Gesta Francorum et aliorum Hierosolimitanorum,* ed. and trans. by Rosalind Hill (London, 1962) in the *Medieval Texts* series. A Muslim view of the Crusading activity of the early twelfth century is presented in Ibn al-Qalanisi's *The Damascus Chronicle of the Crusades,* trans. by Sir H. A. R. Gibb (London, 1932). A Byzantine view of the first Crusade may be found in the *Alexiad* of Anna Comnena, trans. by E. A. S. Dawes (London, 1928).